AIMEE'S PERFECT BAKES

AIMEE'S PERFECT BAKES

Over 50 beautiful bakes and cakes for friends and family

Aimee Twigger

A NOTE FROM AIMEE

I love to cook, but baking has to be my favourite pastime. I love to make cakes and bread for my friends and family, and I get so much joy from seeing people eat something that I have made. I started my blog, Twigg Studios, as a hobby and to share craft projects, but once I began baking and posting my recipes I really found my passion. I didn't expect it to amount to anything, but before I knew it, I was getting an average of 2,000 visitors every day. Now, when I'm not at work, I spend all my time cooking or thinking up new recipes. Baking sweet things is what I love to do most (I have always had a sweet tooth), but I also really enjoy making bread – kneading dough is such a great way to unwind and relieve stress.

This book is laid out so you can easily follow my recipes and enjoy cooking them, rather than being daunted by difficult technical dishes! I have not had any formal training, but I have found trial and error has given me the cooking skills I have today.

After I started sharing my recipes I found that I loved taking photos too – I really enjoy styling and photographing the things I make. I often search in thrift stores for props to style the photos with – eBay is a wonderful place to find beautiful vintage baking equipment; I love to imagine each item has a story behind it. My dad lives in France so I also get a lot of great vintage equipment from there. If I have trouble finding an ingredient on the high street, Amazon can be useful as they have a large food selection and can deliver internationally.

Love, Aimee x

BAKER'S NOTES

Ingredients

Butter: I always use butter at room temperature for cakes and chilled, cubed butter for pastry or cookies.

Baking powder: To check if your baking powder is still active add a spoonful into some water. If it fizzes up, it's still good to use.

Flour: There are so many different types of flour with different gluten levels, such as plain (all-purpose) flour, self-raising flour, spelt flour and rye flour. I tend to use plain or self-raising flour for most of my recipes but I like to use spelt flour, too. Sieve the flour to help prevent any lumps in a batter. When making a cake, always fold in the flour rather than mix it with a hand-held electric beater. When flour is folded in, it doesn't release as much gluten, which helps to make the cake light and fluffy.

Cheese: I generally use strong white cheddar in my savoury baking as I like the flavour, but you can use a milder hard cheese if you prefer.

Nuts: Toast nuts in a preheated oven, 180°C/350°F for 3–5 minutes, to improve the flavour.

Sponges: Un-iced sponges will keep well in the freezer for about 1 month – defrost them completely, then frost them with buttercream.

Equipment

Food processor: I use a food processor for so many things, from making cookie dough and pastry to puréeing fruit and chopping up ingredients. You don't need to waste money investing in an expensive one with loads of attachments, I rarely use any of the attachments except the cutting blade.

Stand mixer: Another kitchen gadget I would recommend is a stand mixer; it is very handy when making meringues or marshmallows.

Rubber spatula: Spatulas are great for folding in mixtures, and they scrape the sides of a bowl very well so everything is mixed properly and there is no waste. A spatula can also be used to spread icing over cakes and cupcakes.

Dough cutter: A dough cutter is handy, I also find it is useful to scrape any dough off the worktop afterwards.

Edible Flowers: These should always be obtained from reputable sources to ensure that they are non-toxic, organic, unsprayed and safe to be consumed. Similarly when selecting blooms or foliage for decoration you should likewise make sure they are unsprayed and organic.

Difficulty Ratings: The difficulty of the recipes is indicated by the oven glove icon, one for easy, two for intermediate and three for the trickier bakes.

CONTENTS

1. Cakes

FEATHER-LIGHT LILAC CAKE

❧❧❧

These wonderful lilacs were given to me from Maddocks Farm Organics here in Devon — they sell fresh edible flowers and seasonal salads and herbs. I decided to infuse the crème pâtissière with the lilacs and a vanilla pod to make the most of their sweet flavour.

The sponge contains no butter or oil and is so light and springy; it's my favourite type of cake and perfect for the delicate flavours.

Feather-light lilac cake

Makes 1 cake / serves 8–10   Difficulty rating

For the crème pâtissière
200 ml (7 fl oz) milk
1 cup of unsprayed/organic
    lilac flowers (about 2 heads)
1 vanilla pod, seeds scraped
2 egg yolks
60 g (2 oz) caster
    (superfine) sugar
20 g (3/4 oz/1 1/2 tablespoons)
    cornflour (cornstarch)

For the cake
4 eggs, separated
115 g (4 oz) caster
    (superfine) sugar
115 g (4 oz) plain
    (all-purpose) flour
1 teaspoon baking powder

To finish
300 ml (10 1/2 fl oz) thick
    (double/heavy) cream
4 tablespoons lemon curd
Fresh unsprayed/organic lilacs,
    to decorate

Equipment
Two 18 cm (6 inch) round cake tins
Baking paper
Wire rack

Prep time: 10 minutes
Baking time: 15–20 minutes

For the crème pâtissière
Put the milk, lilac flowers, vanilla pod and seeds in a pan. Bring to a light boil, remove from the heat, put the lid on and infuse for 10 minutes. In a separate bowl, whisk together the yolks and sugar, then add the cornflour and mix. Pour the mixture through a sieve, then add one-quarter to the yolks and combine. Pour the yolk mixture back into the pan with the remaining milk mixture and stir continuously over a low heat until it thickens. Pour into a bowl and continue to stir to stop any lumps forming.

For the cake
Preheat the oven to 180°C/350°F and grease and line the cake tins. Whip the egg whites until stiff peaks start to form (see figure 1). Slowly add the sugar and whip until thick and glossy (see figure 2). Whisk in the yolks, then sift together the flour and baking powder. Add half to the whites and fold in with a metal spoon (see figure 3) then add the rest, being careful not to lose any of the volume. For the cake sift in half the flour. Spoon into the cake tins (see figure 4) and bake for about 15–20 minutes until golden, well risen and pulling away from the sides of the tins. Leave to cool in the tins for 10 minutes, then remove from the tins and leave to cool on a wire rack.

For the assembly
Spread the crème pâtissière on top of the bottom cake layer, then spread lemon curd onto the bottom of the top layer. Sandwich the layers together. Whip the cream, spoon it onto the top of the cake and spread out. Decorate with lilacs to finish. This cake will keep for 2–3 days in the fridge – remove 30 minutes before serving to come to room temperature.

1. Whip the egg whites for the cake batter until stiff peaks form.

2. Add the sugar and whip until thick and glossy.

3. Fold in the flour using a metal spoon.

4. Spoon the cake batter into the prepared tin.

13

Coconut-coated sponge cake with fruit

Makes 1 cake / serves 8   Difficulty rating

For the cake

220 g (7³/4 oz) butter
 or margarine
220 g (7³/4 oz/1 cup) golden
 caster (superfine) sugar
4 eggs
1 teaspoon vanilla extract
220 g (7³/4 oz) self-raising flour
2¹/2 tablespoons ground almonds
Pinch of salt
45 ml (1¹/2 fl oz) milk

For the decoration

300 ml (10¹/2 fl oz) thick
 (double/heavy) cream
30 g (1 oz/¹/4 cup) icing
 (confectioners') sugar
Drop of vanilla extract
2¹/2 tablespoons raspberry jam
200 g (7 oz/3³/4 cups)
 flaked coconut
Fresh fruit to top the cake

Equipment

Two 18 cm (6 inch) round
 cake tins
Baking paper
Cooling rack
Palette knife

Prep time: 10 minutes
Baking time: 30–35 minutes
Decorating time: 20 minutes

For the cake

Preheat the oven to 180°C/350°F and grease and line 2 cake tins. Cream together the butter and sugar in a bowl until pale. Add the eggs one by one, mixing after each addition. Add the vanilla and mix in. Fold in the flour and ground almonds with a pinch of salt. Add the milk to loosen the batter.

Divide the batter evenly between the two prepared tins and bake for 30–35 minutes until risen and golden. To test use a skewer inserted in the centre of the cake – the cake is ready if it comes out clean. Leave to cool in the tin for 10 minutes, then on a wire rack to cool completely.

For the decorating

Place the cream with the icing sugar and a drop of vanilla extract in a bowl and whip. Spread jam over one of the sponges, top with some whipped cream and spread out evenly. Top with the second sponge.

Use a palette knife to cover the cake with the rest of the whipped cream, then press on some flaked coconut to decorate. Finally, top the cake with your chosen fruit – I used redcurrants, blueberries, blackberries, figs and cherries.

This cake will keep for up to 3 days in the fridge – remove 30 minutes before serving to come to room temperature.

COOKIE DOUGH CHOCOLATE CAKE

This cake is so good, but it is very naughty — it has layers of chocolate cake topped with ganache, cookie dough balls, Oreo crumbs and cheesecake, all in one cake!

I got the idea from Momofuku Milk Bar as their cakes are built up in the same way. It tasted so amazing and is totally worth it. You may need to get some acetate from a craft shop or online for the assembly.

Cookie dough chocolate cake

Makes 1 cake / serves 8–10   *Difficulty rating* 🧤🧤🧤

For the sponge
100 g (3½ oz) dark chocolate,
    broken into pieces
100 g (3½ oz) unsalted butter
65 ml (2 fl oz/¼ cup) milk
Pinch of salt
85 g (3 oz) self-raising flour
110 g (3¾ oz/½ cup) caster
    (superfine) sugar
75 g (2½ oz/⅓ cup) soft light
    brown sugar
2 tablespoons cocoa powder
2 eggs
2½ tablespoons sour cream

For the cookie dough balls
85 g (3 oz) unsalted butter
85 g (3 oz) soft light brown sugar
1 teaspoon vanilla extract
1 tablespoon golden syrup
125 g (4½ oz) plain
    (all-purpose) flour
60 g (2 oz) chocolate chips

continued overleaf ...

Prep time: 40 minutes
Baking time: 35 minutes
Assembly time: 20 minutes
Chilling time: 2 hours

For the sponge
Preheat the oven to 150°C/300°F and grease and line a Swiss roll tin.

Put the chocolate in a pan with the butter and milk and a pinch of salt. Place over a low heat until the chocolate and butter have melted and then set it aside to cool.

Put the flour, sugars and cocoa powder in a bowl and mix together. Add the eggs, mixing them in one at a time. Beat the sour cream into the chocolate mixture, then pour this into the flour mixture and fold together.

Pour the batter into the prepared tin and bake for 35 minutes until a skewer comes out clean. Leave to cool in the tin for 10 minutes and then on a wire rack to cool completely.

For the cookie dough balls
Put the butter and sugar in a food processor and beat together until soft (see figure 1).

Add the vanilla and golden syrup (see figure 2) and mix together. Add the flour and chocolate chips and mix together into a dough (see figure 3).

Roll small lumps of the dough into small balls (see figure 4) and place them on a cookie sheet.

1. Beat the sugar and butter together to make the cookie dough balls.

2. Add the vanilla and golden syrup and beat together.

3. Add the flour and chocolate chips and mix into a dough.

4. Roll small lumps of dough into tiny balls ready to layer the cake.

5. Create a cylinder out of a sheet of acetate.

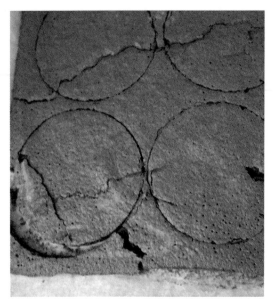

6. Cut at least 3 layers of sponge from your cooked sponge sheet.

7. Start to assemble the cake by layering sponge, cheesecake, ganache and cookie dough balls.

8. The layered cake.

For the cheesecake

120 ml (4 fl oz / $1/2$ cup) thick
   (double/heavy) cream
50 g ($13/4$ oz) icing
   (confectioners') sugar
170 g (6 oz/$2/3$ cup)
   cream cheese
1 teaspoon vanilla extract

For the ganache

120 ml (4 fl oz/$1/2$ cup) thick
   (double/heavy) cream
45 g ($11/2$ oz/$21/2$ tablespoons)
   butter
100 g ($31/2$ oz) dark chocolate,
   broken into pieces

To decorate

7 Oreo cookies, crumbled

Equipment

20 x 30 cm (8 x 12 inch) Swiss
   roll tin
Cookie sheet
Sheet of acetate large enough
   to make a 12.5 cm (5 inch) cake
Piping bag

For the cheesecake

Whip the cream and icing sugar together in a bowl until thick, then add the cream cheese and vanilla extract and whip together.

For the ganache

Heat the cream and butter in a saucepan over a gentle heat, bring to the boil, then take off the heat and stir in the chocolate until it has melted. Leave to cool until slightly thickened.

For the assembly

Take a sheet of acetate and make a cylinder to fit a 12.5 cm (5 inch) cake tin (see figure 5). Cut the sponge to fit inside – I have a really large pastry cutter the same size as I made the cylinder, so used that (see figure 6). You will need to cut at least 3 pieces from the sponge.

Put the first sponge layer into the bottom of the cylinder and then start layering up. First add one-quarter of the cheesecake layer, then pour in one-third of the ganache. Add one-third of the crushed Oreo cookies and one-third of the cookie dough balls (see figure 7).

Add the next layer of sponge and continue layering up again with the next sequence of layers. Repeat with the third layer of sponge (see figure 8).

To finish, spoon the last of the cheesecake mixture into a piping bag and pipe onto the top of the cake. Add some Oreo crumbs and the cookie dough balls. Chill for 2 hours, then carefully peel away the acetate before serving.

This cake will keep well for 2–3 days in the fridge – remove 30 minutes before serving to come to room temperature.

Beetroot chocolate cake

Makes 1 cake / serves 8–10   Difficulty rating

Prep time: 20 minutes (plus 1 1/2 hours to cook the beets)
Baking time: 50 minutes
Decoration time: 10 minutes

For the cake
200 g (7 oz) dark chocolate
200 g (7 oz) unsalted butter
200 g (7 oz) soft light
   brown sugar
4 eggs separated
200 g (7 oz) beetroot, cooked
   and puréed (about 3 beets)
140 g (5 oz) self-raising flour
3 tablespoons cocoa powder

For the frosting
100 g (3 1/2 oz) dark chocolate
400 g (14 oz) unsalted butter
200 g (7 oz)
   icing (confectioners') sugar
3 tablespoons cocoa powder

For the decoration
Unsprayed/organic fresh
   flowers to top the cake

Equipment
Two 18 cm (6 inch) round
   cake tins
Food processor
Cooling rack

For the cake
Preheat the oven to 170°C/325°F and grease two round cake tins. Melt the chocolate in a heatproof bowl set over a pan of boiling water (making sure the water doesn't touch the base of the bowl), then leave it to cool for 5 minutes.

Put the butter and 150 g (5 1/2 oz) of the sugar and cream together in a bowl and beat until soft and fluffy. Add the egg yolks and mix through. Put the egg whites and remaining 50 g (1 3/4 oz) of sugar in a separate clean bowl and whisk until stiff peaks form. Add the beetroot purée to the chocolate and mix, then add that to the butter mixture. Sift in the flour and cocoa powder. Add one-quarter of the egg white mixture to the chocolate mixture to loosen it, then fold the rest in gently.

Pour the batter into two greased baking tins and bake for about 45–50 minutes. Test each cake is cooked by inserting a skewer into the centre, if it comes out clean it is done. Leave to cool in the tins for 10 minutes, then on a wire rack to cool completely.

For the frosting
Melt the chocolate over a pan of boiling water, then leave it to cool for a few minutes. Beat the butter until soft, then add the icing sugar and cocoa and mix. Mix in the melted chocolate.

Spread half the frosting on top of one of the sponges and spread out evenly. Top with the second sponge and spread the remaining frosting over the top. Keep in an airtight container and eat within 3–4 days.

RASPBERRY RIPPLE CAKE

I created this cake for my grandma's birthday because she loves raspberries. The sponge tastes just like a raspberry and white chocolate muffin.

I don't use loads of sugar in the frosting so it's sweet but not overly sweet and tastes light and not sickly. It's perfect for after a birthday meal when you only have enough room left for a sliver. Everyone sitting at the table for the birthday meal asked for the recipe, so it must be a winner!

Raspberry ripple cake

Makes 1 cake / serves 8–10   *Difficulty rating* 🧤🧤🧤

Prep time: 20 minutes
Baking time: 30–40 minutes
Decoration time: 30 minutes

For the sponge
220 g (7³/₄ oz) butter
220 g (8 oz/1 cup) caster
  (superfine) sugar
4 eggs
1 teaspoon vanilla extract
220 g (8 oz)
  self-raising flour
Pinch of salt
30 ml (1 fl oz) milk
75 g (2³/₄ oz) white chocolate,
  chopped into small chunks
100 g (3¹/₂ oz) raspberries

For the frosting
100 g (3¹/₂ oz) raspberries
50 g (1³/₄ oz) icing
  (confectioners') sugar
900 ml (31 fl oz/3¹/₂ cups) thick
  (double/heavy) cream
250 g (9 oz) cream cheese
1 teaspoon vanilla extract

To assemble
Raspberry jam, for spreading
Pink food colouring gel

Equipment
Three 15 cm (6 inch) cake tins
Paintbrush
Piping bag

Preheat the oven to 180°C/350°F and grease and line the cake tins. Cream together the butter and sugar in a bowl until soft and pale. Add the eggs, one at a time, stirring after each addition. Add the vanilla extract and mix, then add the flour and salt and fold in with a spatula. Add the milk to loosen the batter, then add the white chocolate chunks and stir in the fresh raspberries. Spoon the batter into the prepared cake tins and bake for 30–40 minutes. Once cooked, leave to cool completely.

For the frosting
Put the raspberries and 2 tablespoons of the icing sugar in a pan and heat until they become juicy. Mash with a spoon, then push through a sieve to remove the seeds. Leave to cool. Whip the cream and remaining icing sugar together in a bowl until thick, then add the raspberry purée, cream cheese and vanilla.

To assemble
Level the cakes by slicing off any risen parts. Add a tablespoon of raspberry jam to the bottom sponge, smooth out, then add some frosting and place another sponge on top. Repeat until all sponges are used. Smooth frosting evenly over the cake (see figure 1). Paint food colouring lines on the inside of a piping bag (see figure 2). Spoon the rest of the frosting into the bag. Pipe small circles in a vertical line down the side of the cake (see figure 3). Take a palette knife and drag each one across to make a smudge. Pipe another line of circles next to them (see figure 4). Continue around the cake until the sides are covered and do the same on top in a circular motion. This cake will keep for 2–3 days in the fridge (remove 30 minutes before serving).

1. Cover the whole cake in a thin, even layer of frosting.

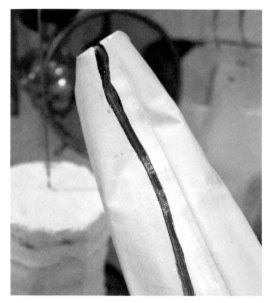

2. Paint a couple of lines of pink colouring inside the piping bag, then fill with frosting.

3. Pipe a vertical line of small circles down the side of the cake.

4. Use a palette knife to drag each circle to the slide slightly to create a smudge and then pipe another line of circles next to them.

Blackberry and apple crêpe cake

Makes 1 cake / serves 6   Difficulty rating 🧤🧤

For the crêpes
120 ml (4 fl oz/^{1}/$_2$ cup) water
120 ml (4 fl oz/^{1}/$_2$ cup) milk
2 eggs
140 g (5 oz) plain
    (all-purpose) flour
1 tablespoon caster
    (superfine) sugar
^{1}/$_2$ teaspoon ground cinnamon
3 apples
2 tablespoons soft light
    brown sugar
1 teaspoon butter
220 g (8 oz) blackberries

For the lavender caramel
60 g (2 oz/^{1}/$_4$ cup) butter
Few drops of lavender extract
60 g (2 oz/^{1}/$_3$ cup) soft light
    brown sugar
30 ml (1 fl oz) thick
    (double/heavy) cream

For the blackberry cream
350 ml (12 fl oz) thick
    (double/heavy) cream
40 g (1^1/$_2$ oz/^{1}/$_3$ cup) icing
    (confectioners') sugar,
    plus a little extra for dusting
100 g (3^1/$_2$ oz/^{3}/$_4$ cup)
    blackberries

Equipment
Baking sheet
Piping bag

Prep time: 10 minutes
Cooking time: 30 minutes
Assembly time: 15 minutes

For the crêpes
Whisk the water and milk with the eggs in a bowl and then add the flour, sugar and cinnamon and mix until smooth. Put in the fridge for 20 minutes to chill. Preheat the oven to 180°C/350°F. Thinly slice the apples, spread them out on a baking sheet and sprinkle over some brown sugar. Bake for 10–15 minutes until soft.

Heat a pan and add the butter, then pour in about 3 tablespoons of batter. Tip the pan to spread the batter around. Cook for 1 minute, then flip over and cook on the other side for another 30 seconds until it turns golden. Set aside and continue with the rest of the mixture (you should make about 8–10 crêpes).

For the lavender caramel
Put the butter, lavender extract and sugar in a microwaveable bowl, heat for 1 minute in the microwave, then stir until the sugar dissolves. Heat again for 20 seconds, then leave to cool a little. Stir in the cream.

For the blackberry cream
Put the cream in a bowl with the icing sugar and whip until thick. Add the blackberries and mix gently to break the fruit up.

To assemble
Put a crêpe on a serving platter and pipe on some blackberry cream. Add some apples and blackberries, then drizzle over some caramel. Continue adding layers until all the crêpes are used up. Finish with some blackberries on top, drizzle over some more caramel, then dust with icing sugar. Best eaten the same day.

'RAINBOW' CAKE WITH EDIBLE FLOWERS

I wanted to create a rainbow cake with natural flavours and colours rather than using food colouring. I asked the florist for a rainbow selection of edible flowers to go with the cake; I was so pleased with the beautiful selection they sent.

'Rainbow' cake with edible flowers

Makes 1 cake / serves 8–10   Difficulty rating

For the red layer
70 g (2¹/₂ oz) strawberries,
   chopped (reserving a few
   chopped strawberries)
1 tablespoon water
30 g (1 oz) caster
   (superfine) sugar
1 teaspoon beetroot powder
   (beetroot juice also works well)

For the green layer
1 teaspoon matcha green
   tea powder

For the orange layer
Zest of 1 orange and
   1 tablespoon of juice
1 carrot, cooked and puréed

For the yellow layer
Zest of 1 lemon and juice
   of half a lemon

For the blue layer
100 g (3¹/₂ oz/²/₃ cup)
   blueberries, plus
   8 whole blueberries
1 tablespoon water
30 g (1 oz) caster
   (superfine) sugar

continued overleaf ...

Prep time: 30 minutes
Baking time: 25 minutes per cake layer
Decoration time: 20 minutes

Prepare the flavourings
Make the fruit purées. Put the blueberries and chopped strawberries into two separate pans with the water and sugar and reduce until you get a thick liquid. Strain through a sieve into separate bowls and leave to cool.

For the cake
Preheat the oven to 180°C/350°F and then grease and line the cake tins.

Cream together the butter and sugar until pale and fluffy. Add 2 of the eggs. Separate the yolks from the other 2 eggs and keep to one side, but add the whites to the mixture and continue mixing. Add the vanilla extract and then fold in the flour. Separate the mixture equally into 5 different bowls.

Add the flavourings
Add the strawberry purée and beetroot powder (which should be available to buy online or from healthfood stores) to one bowl and add the reserved chopped strawberries (see figure 1). Mix together.

Add the matcha green tea powder to another portion and then mix together.

Add one of the reserved egg yolks to another bowl, with the puréed carrot and grated orange zest and juice, and mix together (see figure 2).

1. Add the flavourings for the red layer to the first bowl of cake mixture.

2. Add the flavourings for the orange layer to another bowl of cake mixture.

3. Continue with the flavourings and colourings for all of the layers.

4. The five different flavoured and coloured cake batters mixed and ready to add to tins.

5. Keep layering with frosting until you have used all of the coloured cake layers.

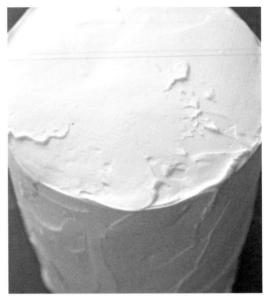

6. Use a palette knife to cover the cake in frosting.

7. Choose flowers in a range of colours that will create a confetti effect on the cake.

8. Press the flowers all over the cake to finish.

For the cake
220 g (7³/₄ oz) unsalted butter
220 g (8 oz/1 cup) caster
   (superfine) sugar
4 eggs
1 teaspoon vanilla extract
220 g (8 oz)
   self-raising flour

For the frosting
400 ml (14 fl oz) thick
   (double/heavy) cream
100 g (3¹/₂ oz) cream cheese
50 g (1³/₄ oz) icing
   (confectioners') sugar
30 g unsprayed/organic
   edible flowers (such as
   borage or violas)

Equipment
Five 23 cm (9 inch)
   round cake tins
Baking paper
5 mixing bowls
Palette knife

Add the other reserved egg yolk to another bowl with the lemon zest and juice to make the yellow layer.

Add the blueberry purée to the final bowl of batter and add some more whole blueberries.

You should now have 5 different coloured bowls of cake batter (see figures 3 and 4).

Add the batter to the prepared tins and bake for about 25 minutes. To check the cakes are cooked, insert a skewer into the centre. If it come out clean then the cake is cooked. Leave to cool while you make the frosting.

For the frosting
Whip the cream with the icing sugar in a bowl until thick, then add the cream cheese. Add more icing sugar depending on how sweet you like it.

Spread some frosting between each layer of sponge and build it up into a tall cake (see figure 5). I started with purple, then pink, orange, yellow and green.

Use a spatula to cover the cake with frosting (see figure 6), then add the flowers like colourful confetti (see figure 8).

This cake will keep well for 2–3 days in the fridge – remove 30 minutes before serving to come to room temperature.

TIRAMISU CAKE WITH HAZELNUT DACQUOISE

I made this tiramisu as a treat for my partner. I decided
to make it a little different by using layers of hazelnut
meringue as well as homemade lady finger biscuits.
I don't usually like coffee, but for some reason I really
love it in this dessert.

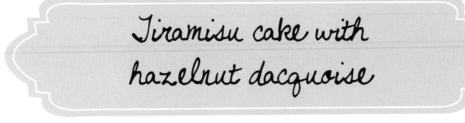

Tiramisu cake with hazelnut dacquoise

Makes 1 cake / serves 8   Difficulty rating

For the hazelnut dacquoise
125 g (4 1/2 oz) hazelnuts
20 g (3/4 oz/1 1/2 tablespoons)
    cornflour (cornstarch)
150 g (5 1/2 oz/2/3 cup) caster
    (superfine) sugar
3 egg whites
1/2 teaspoon salt

For the syrup
100 g (3 1/2 oz) granulated sugar
1 teaspoon coffee granules
1 tablespoon cocoa powder
100 ml (3 1/2 fl oz) water
1/2 teaspoon vanilla extract

continued overleaf ...

Prep time: 30 minutes
Baking time: 1 hour and 5 minutes
Assembly time: 10 minutes

For the hazelnut dacquoise
Preheat the oven to 180°C (350°F). Line 2 trays with baking paper and draw three 15 cm (6 inch) circles on the paper (2 on one tray, 1 on the other, see figure 1).

Chop the hazelnuts in a food processor until coarse, then spread them out onto a baking sheet. Bake for 3 minutes, then stir and bake again for a further 3 minutes. Stir again, then bake for a final 3 minutes. Turn the oven down to 150°C/300°F.

Put the roasted hazelnuts in a bowl, mix in the cornflour and 50 g (1 3/4 oz) of the sugar and set aside.

Put the egg whites in the bowl of a stand mixer and use the whisk attachment to beat them at a medium speed for about 2 minutes or until frothy. Add the remaining sugar as it is mixing, turn up the speed and beat until stiff peaks form and you can tip the bowl upside down without the meringue falling out.

Add the nut/sugar mixture and fold in (see figure 2). Pipe the meringue mixture onto the paper to cover the 3 circles (see figure 3), then bake for 1 hour. Move the trays around halfway through baking so that they bake equally.

For the syrup
Put all the syrup ingredients in a pan over a medium heat and stir to combine. Bring to the boil and leave the syrup to reduce so it thickens slightly. Pour into a bowl ready for dipping.

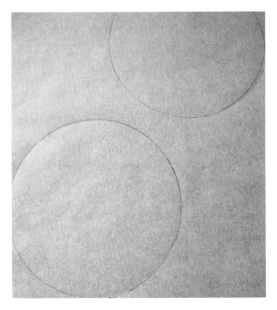

1. Draw 3 circles on baking paper ready for piping the meringue.

2. Mix the roasted hazelnuts into the meringue mixture.

3. Pipe the meringue mixture over the drawn circles to create the dacquoise discs.

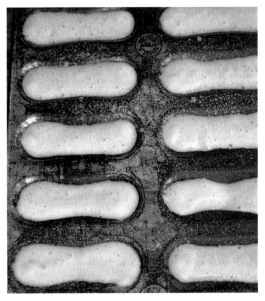

4. Use an eclair pan to bake the biscuits or alternatively, just pipe long fingers onto a lined baking tray.

For the lady finger biscuits

2 eggs

50 g (1³/4 oz) caster
  (superfine) sugar

¹/2 teaspoon vanilla extract

75 g (2³/4 oz/¹/2 cup)
  self-raising flour

For the cream

200 ml (7 fl oz) thick
  (double/heavy) cream

300 g (10¹/2 oz/1¹/4 cups)
  mascarpone

50 g (1³/4 oz) icing
  (confectioners') sugar

1 teaspoon vanilla extract

To finish

Cocoa powder, to dust

Equipment

Food processor

Baking sheet

2 baking trays

Baking paper

Piping bags

Cookie sheet or eclair pan

For the lady finger biscuits

Preheat the oven to 200°C/400°F.

Put the eggs, sugar and vanilla in a bowl and whip for about 5 minutes or until thick, creamy and pale. Sift in the flour and fold through. Spoon into a piping bag and pipe fingers about 15 cm (6 inches) long onto a cookie sheet or into an eclair pan (see figure 4) and bake for 5 minutes until springy to the touch (see figure 5). Leave to cool, then dip them in the syrup (see figure 6).

For the cream

Whip the cream until thick and then stir through the mascarpone, icing sugar and vanilla extract. Spoon into a piping bag ready for piping.

To assemble

Put one hazelnut dacquoise layer on a serving plate or stand. Pipe a layer of cream on top and then cover with soaked lady fingers (these can be cut to fit as necessary, see figures 7 and 8). Add another layer of dacquoise, then cream and then lady fingers and top with a final layer of hazelnut dacquoise. Pipe some cream on top and dust with cocoa powder to finish. Best eaten straight away.

5. The baked lady fingers.

6. Dip the lady fingers in the coffee syrup before getting ready to assemble the cake.

7. Pipe a layer of cream on top of the base dacquoise layer.

8. Top the cream with soaked lady fingers.

Persimmon cinnamon cake

Makes 1 cake / serves 8–10   *Difficulty rating*

For the sponge
200 g (7 oz) soft light
  brown sugar
100 g (3^1/$_2$ oz) caster
  (superfine) sugar
300 g (10^1/$_2$ oz) unsalted butter
5 eggs
1 teaspoon vanilla extract
300 g (10^1/$_2$ oz/2 cups)
  self-raising flour
2 teaspoons ground cinnamon
30 ml (1 fl oz) milk
1 persimmon

For the frosting
600 ml (21 fl oz) thick
  (double/heavy) cream
80 g (2 ^{3}/$_4$ oz) icing
  (confectioners') sugar
200 g (7 oz) cream cheese
1 tablespoon vanilla extract
1 persimmon, sliced, and
  unsprayed/organic edible
  leaves (such as bay leaves)
  to decorate

Equipment
Two 15 cm (6 inch) round
  cake tins
Wire rack

Preparation time: 20 minutes
Baking time: 50 minutes
Decorating time: 10 minutes

For the sponge
Preheat the oven to 180°C/350°F, grease and line the cake tins.

Put the sugars and butter in a bowl and beat together until soft and fluffy. Add the eggs one at a time, making sure each one is properly combined before adding the next. Add the vanilla extract and mix in. Add the flour and cinnamon and fold through. To loosen the batter, add a little milk.

Chop the persimmon into small chunks and stir it through the batter. Spoon the batter evenly into the two prepared tins and bake for 45–50 minutes. To test, insert a skewer into the centre; if it comes out clean the cake is cooked. Leave to cool in the tin for 10 minutes, then on a wire rack to cool completely.

For the frosting
Whip the cream and icing sugar until thick, then add the vanilla extract and cream cheese and mix well.

To assemble
Slice the sponges in half horizontally. Place one sponge layer on a cake plate and spread over some frosting. Add another sponge layer and continue building up the cake. Frost the cake with 'dirty icing' (see page 49) and decorate with persimmon slices and edible leaves such as bay. This cake will keep for up to 3 days in the fridge – remove 30 minutes before serving to come to room temperature.

MANDARIN LEMON CAKE WITH CREAM CHEESE FROSTING

❧❀☙

I found some mandarins at the supermarket and decided to make this cake. It's great for celebrations as lemon and orange flavours are always a hit and tiered cakes cannot help but look special.

Mandarin lemon cake with cream cheese frosting

Makes one 2-tiered cake / serves 10–15   Difficulty rating

For the cake

700 g (12 oz/4²/₃ cups) plain
(all-purpose) flour
6 teaspoons baking powder
2 teaspoons bicarbonate of soda
(baking soda)
Pinch of salt
450 g (1 lb) unsalted butter
700 g (1 lb 8 oz) caster
(superfine) sugar
8 large eggs
2 teaspoons vanilla extract
Juice and zest of 2 mandarins
Zest of 2 lemons and juice
of 1 lemon
500 ml (17 fl oz/2 cups) buttermilk

For the buttercream and layering the cake

450 g (1 lb) unsalted butter
300 g (10 ½ oz) icing
(confectioners') sugar
Juice and zest of 2 lemons
Zest of 2 mandarins
600 g (1 lb 5 oz) lemon curd

continued overleaf ...

Prep time: 20 minutes
Baking time: 50 minutes
Decoration time: 20 minutes

For the cakes

Preheat the oven to 180°C/350°F and then grease and line all the cake tins.

Sift together the flour, baking powder, bicarbonate of soda and salt.

Cream together the butter and sugar until thick and pale. Lightly beat the eggs and vanilla and gradually add them to the mixture, mixing well between each addition. Add the juice and zest of the mandarin and lemon and mix in.

Stir in the dry ingredients and buttermilk, alternating between the two. Once the batter is mixed, divide it between each lined tin. Bake the larger cakes for 30 minutes and the smaller cakes for 25 minutes. Once cooked, turn the sponges out onto a wire rack to cool, then slice the tops off the sponges so that they are level.

For the buttercream

Cream the butter until softened, then sift in the icing sugar. Add the lemon and mandarin zest and juice and mix through.

Spread the top of one of the large sponges with lemon curd, then buttercream. Top with the other large sponge and repeat with the smaller sponges so you have two separate filled cakes (see figure 1).

1. Sandwich the larger cake with buttercream and then top with frosting.

2. Spread the frosting all over this base tier so that it is evenly covered.

3. Use a palette knife to smooth the frosting, aiming for a slightly rustic finish.

4. Position the smaller cake on top and use wooden dowels to secure. Cut off any excess.

5. Top with more frosting.

6. Use a palette knife to smooth it all over.

7. Use a smaller knife to keep smoothing to create a flawless finish.

8. Top with a mandarin and your choice of fresh flowers.

For the frosting

1 litre (34 fl oz/4 cups) thick
    (double/heavy) cream
100 g (3$\frac{1}{2}$ oz) icing
    (confectioners') sugar
360 g (12 oz/1$\frac{1}{2}$ cups)
    cream cheese
2 teaspoons vanilla extract
Few drops of peach or orange
    food colouring
1 mandarin and unsprayed/
    organic edible leaves and
    flowers to decorate

Equipment

Two 18 cm (6 inch) round
    cake tins
Two 23 cm (9 inch) round
    cake tins

For the frosting

Whip the cream and icing sugar together until stiff peaks form, then add the cream cheese, vanilla and food colouring.

To assemble

Ideally, to stop the crumbs getting in the frosting, you would cover both cakes in a thin layer of frosting first, before you layer the cakes. This is called 'dirty icing'.

Use a palette knife to spread frosting on top of the larger cake, bringing frosting over the edge and down the sides. Smooth and level out.

Position the smaller cake on top and push some wooden dowels all the way down through both cakes. Cut off the excess dowel. Add frosting to the top of the small cake and, as before, take the frosting down over the sides and smooth out using the palette knife.

Continue smoothing until the whole tiered cake is as smooth as possible (see figures 2 to 7). I like the rustic look of the frosting rather than a sharp edge. Decorate as you wish – I used a mandarin, flowers and lavender.

This cake will keep well for 2–3 days in the fridge – remove 30 minutes before serving to come to room temperature.

Victoria sponge cake

Makes 1 2-tiered cake / serves 10   *Difficulty rating*

For the cake

285 g (10 oz) unsalted butter
285 g (10 oz) caster
    (superfine) sugar
5 eggs
1 teaspoon vanilla extract
285 g (10 oz) plain
    (all-purpose) flour
2 teaspoons baking powder

For the filling and layering the cake

400 ml (14 fl oz) thick
    (double/heavy) cream
40 g (1^1/$_2$ oz/^{1}/$_3$ cup) icing
    (confectioners') sugar, plus
    extra for dusting
Raspberry jam, for spreading
Raspberries and candied rose
    petals, to decorate

Equipment

Two 23 cm (9 inch) round
    cake tins
Two 28 cm (11 inch) round
    cake tins

Prep time: 10 minutes
Baking time: 35–40 minutes
Decorating time: 20 minutes

Preheat the oven to 180°C/350°F and then grease and line the cake tins.

Cream the butter and sugar together for about 3 minutes until thick and pale. Add the eggs one at a time, making sure each one is incorporated before adding the next. Add the vanilla extract, sift in the flour and baking powder and fold in with a spatula.

Pour the batter into the prepared tins and bake the smaller cakes for 30 minutes and the larger ones for 35–40 minutes. To check each cake is cooked, insert a skewer into the centre and if it comes out clean the cake is done. Leave to cool in the tin for 10 minutes, then on a wire rack to cool completely.

Whip the cream with the icing sugar until almost stiff.

Starting with the largest layers, spread jam onto a layer of sponge and add the cream on top. Level out and add the next cake layer. Repeat with the smaller cake and add on top, securing in place with cake dowels (see page 47).

Sift over icing sugar and decorate with raspberries and candied rose petals.

This cake will keep well for 2–3 days in the fridge – remove 30 minutes before serving to come to room temperature.

No 3

Parsnip pear cake

Makes 1 cake / serves 8   *Difficulty rating* 🧤

For the cake
320 g (11 oz) unsalted butter,
    melted and cooled
320 g (11 oz) soft light
    brown sugar
4 eggs
320 g (11 oz) plain
    (all-purpose) flour
2 teaspoons bicarbonate
    of soda (baking soda)
1 teaspoon ground cinnamon
Pinch of salt
100 g ($3^1/_2$ oz) peeled and
    grated parsnip
200 g (7 oz) peeled and
    chopped pears
$^1/_2$ tablespoon finely chopped
    rosemary, and sprigs to decorate

For the buttercream
125 g ($4^1/_2$ oz) unsalted butter
200 g (7 oz) icing
    (confectioners') sugar
2 teaspoons ground cinnamon
50 ml ($1^1/_2$ fl oz) thick
    (double/heavy) cream

Equipment
Two 15 cm (6 inch) round
    cake tins
Baking paper
Wire rack
Stand mixer or handheld
    electric mixer

Prep time: 20 minutes
Baking time: 40–50 minutes
Decorating time: 20 minutes

For the cake
Preheat the oven to 170°C/335°F and grease and line the cake tins.

Use a stand mixer or handheld electric mixer to beat the butter, sugar and eggs together for 2 minutes until pale and well combined. Sift together the flour, bicarbonate of soda and salt together in a clean bowl. Add the flour mixture to the butter mixture and fold to combine by hand.

Finally, fold in the parsnip, pear and rosemary and divide the batter between the two tins. Bake for 40–50 minutes until a skewer inserted in the centre comes out clean. Leave to cool on a wire rack.

For the buttercream
Use a stand mixer or handheld electric mixer to beat the butter for 3–4 minutes until pale and creamy, then add the icing sugar, cinnamon and cream and mix until smooth.

To assemble
Level the cakes by cutting off the domed tops and slice each cake in two so you have four layers. Place one layer on a cake plate, spoon (or pipe) on the buttercream. Add another layer and continue to add more buttercream until you get to the top layer. Finish with a layer of buttercream on the top and decorate with rosemary. This cake will keep for 2–3 days in the fridge – remove 30 minutes before serving to come to room temperature.

DOMINICAN(ISH) CAKE WITH ROSE AND LIME

This cake is based on a typical Dominican cake. The first time I travelled to the Dominican Republic was for my 21st birthday and it was also the first holiday my partner and I took together. He was obsessed with the white frosting on the cakes there and always went back for a second slice. So I made this cake for him.

Dominican (ish) cake with rose and lime

Makes 1 cake / serves 8–10   Difficulty rating 🧤

Prep time: 10 minutes
Baking time: 50 minutes
Icing time: 15 minutes

For the sponge

300 g (10 1/2 oz/2 cups) plain
   (all purpose) flour, plus extra
   for dusting
15 g (1/2 oz) baking powder
1 teaspoon fine grain sea salt
225 g (8 oz) unsalted butter, plus
   extra for greasing
200 g (7 oz) granulated sugar
4 large eggs, plus 1 yolk at
   room temperature
120 ml (4 fl oz/1/2 cup) milk
2 teaspoons pure vanilla extract

For the filling and frosting

120 ml (4 fl oz/1/2 cup) egg whites
   (about 4 large eggs)
200 g (7 oz) granulated sugar
Juice of 1/2 a lime
2 teaspoons pure vanilla extract
30 ml (1 fl oz) rosewater
1/4 teaspoon sea salt
3 tablespoons lime curd, to fill

Equipment

Two 18 cm (6 inch) round
   cake tins
Baking paper
Stand mixer or handheld
   electric mixer
Saucepan

For the cake

Preheat the oven to 180°C/350°F and grease and line the round cake tins, then butter the baking paper and dust with flour; tap out the excess. Sift together the flour, baking powder and salt and set aside.

Use a stand mixer fitted with the paddle on medium speed to beat the butter and sugar for 6 minutes until pale and creamy, scraping down the side of the bowl every now and then. Add the eggs and yolks one at a time. Mix in the milk and vanilla. Sift in the flour mixture and mix just until the flour is no longer visible. Evenly divide between the two tins and level out. Bake for 45–50 minutes until golden brown and a skewer comes out clean. Leave to cool, level the cakes, then make the frosting.

For the frosting

Fit a large heatproof bowl over a pan of simmering water (do not let the water touch the bowl). Put all the ingredients in the bowl with 3 tablespoons water (see figure 1) and whisk constantly for about 3–4 minutes or until the sugar has dissolved and the mixture looks satiny (see figure 2). Pour into the bowl of a stand mixer with a whisk attachment and mix for 6–8 minutes or until stiff and glossy (see figure 3).

Spoon some lime curd onto one sponge, then top with the other sponge. Spread a thick layer of frosting all over the cake (see figure 4). This cake will keep for 2–3 days in the fridge – remove 30 minutes before serving.

1. Put all the ingredients for the frosting in a heatproof bowl set over a pan of simmering water.

2. Whisk the mixture for 3–4 minutes until the sugar has dissolved.

3. Transfer the mixture to the bowl of a stand mixer and whisk until stiff and glossy.

4. Use the frosting to sandwich the two cakes together and spoon a large dollop on top and smooth all around the cake to cover it.

2. Sweet bakes

HOT CROSS BUNS

Hot cross buns are made from enriched dough and are traditionally eaten on Good Friday, but they are so delicious I could eat them all the time. I love the cinnamon spice, the orange zest and dried fruit flavours together.
I like to slice them in half, toast them and spread butter on while they are still hot.

Hot cross buns

Makes 10   Difficulty rating

For the buns

150 ml (5 fl oz) milk, plus
  2 tablespoons for brushing
30 g (1 oz) unsalted butter
Zest of 1 orange
1 small egg, beaten
250 g (9 oz/1²/₃ cups)
  strong white flour
60 g (2 oz) caster
  (superfine) sugar
1 teaspoon ground cinnamon
¹/₂ teaspoon salt
7 g (2 teaspoons) fast-action
  dried yeast
60 g (2 oz/¹/₃ cup) sultanas
  or mixed dried fruit
3 tablespoons mixed peel

For the cross

75 g (2³/₄ oz/¹/₂ cup) plain
  (all-purpose) flour, plus
  extra for dusting
2–3 tablespoons water

For the glaze

2–3 tablespoons apricot jam

Equipment

Baking tin
Baking paper
Piping bag fitted with a small
  nozzle
Pastry brush

Prep time: 25 minutes, plus 3–4 hours proving
Baking time: 30 minutes

For the buns

Heat the milk in a pan over a gentle heat and stir in the butter until it melts. Grate in the orange zest, leave to cool for 5–10 minutes, then add the beaten egg. Put the flour, sugar, cinnamon, salt, and yeast in a bowl, making sure to keep the salt and yeast apart (if they touch the yeast may be deactivated) and mix. Add the milk and egg mixture and mix until it all comes together. Lightly dust a clean worktop with flour and tip out the dough. Knead for 5 minutes – the dough will be wet and hard to work at first. Place the dough in an oiled bowl and cover with plastic wrap. Leave to rise for 1–2 hours or until it has doubled in size.

Mix the dried fruit and peel in a bowl. Tip the dough onto a floured worktop and sprinkle over the dried fruit. Knead it into the dough so that it is well distributed. Cover and set aside for 1 hour, or until doubled in size (see figure 1). Divide the dough into 6 pieces (see figure 2) and roll into balls. Place in a circle on a piece of baking paper or in a lined baking tin, leaving a gap between each ball of dough (see figure 3). Loosely cover with oiled plastic wrap and leave to prove for 1 hour.

For the cross

Preheat the oven to 200°C/400°F. Brush the buns with a little milk. Mix the flour with the water (adding a tablespoon of water at a time) and stir it into a paste. Place the paste in the piping bag and pipe the crosses on top of the buns (see figure 4). Bake for 20–25 minutes until golden brown. Heat the apricot jam in a pan over a gentle heat and brush it over the buns to glaze. Leave to cool. These buns are best eaten the same day, but will keep for 1–2 days in an airtight container.

1. The risen dough.

2. Divide the dough into 6 equal pieces.

3. Place the dough balls in a lined tin and leave to rise for 1 hour.

4. Pipe a cross on each bun before baking.

Lime and coconut madeleines

Makes 20   Difficulty rating

For the madeleines
80 g (2³/₄ oz/¹/₄ cup)
    granulated sugar
90 g (3¹/₄ oz) self-raising flour
1 teaspoon baking powder
60 g (2 oz/¹/₄ cup) unsalted
    butter, plus a little extra melted
    butter for brushing
2 eggs
40 g (1¹/₂ oz) desiccated
    (shredded) coconut
1 teaspoon runny honey
Zest of 1 lime

For the coating
3 tablespoons granulated sugar
3 tablespoons desiccated
    (shredded) coconut
1 teaspoon grated lime zest

Equipment
Two 9-hole madeleine moulds

Prep time: 10 minutes
Chilling time: 1 hour
Baking time: 6–8 minutes

For the madeleines
Put the flour, sugar and baking powder in a mixing bowl. Melt the butter in a small saucepan over a gentle heat, let it cool a little, then add it to the bowl.

Add the eggs and mix in. Add the coconut and honey and grate the zest of 1 lime into the bowl. Mix everything together until evenly combined. Cover and put in the fridge for at least 1 hour.

Brush the madeleine moulds with a little melted butter, then sift over some flour. Turn the moulds over and tap out any excess flour. Put the moulds in the fridge to harden the butter for about 10 minutes.

Preheat the oven to 200°C/400°F.

Spoon the mixture evenly into the moulds, then tap each tray on the side to spread out the mixture. Bake for 6–8 minutes.

For the coating
Put the coating ingredients together in a shallow tray and mix. Once the madeleines are cooked and while they are still warm, remove them from the moulds and roll them in the coating until they are evenly covered. They are best eaten the same day but can be kept in an airtight container for 2–4 days.

LEMON POPPY SEED ROLLS

Lemon is one of my favourite ingredients in sweet recipes. I had a few lemons that needed using up, so I made these lemon rolls and they were so good. My dad was visiting from France and insisted on taking a few with him when he left.

Lemon poppy seed rolls

Makes 8   Difficulty rating 🧤🧤

For the dough

500 g (1 lb 2 oz/3¹/₃ cups) strong
   white flour, plus extra to dust
¹/₂ teaspoon salt
7 g (2 teaspoons) fast-action
   dried yeast
15 g (¹/₂ oz/3 teaspoons) caster
   (superfine) sugar
40 g (1¹/₂ oz/2 tablespoons)
   unsalted butter, softened
1 small egg, beaten
100 ml (3¹/₂ fl oz) milk
200 ml (7 fl oz) warm water
2–3 tablespoons poppy seeds

For the filling

60 g (2 oz/¹/₄ cup) butter
60 g (2 oz/¹/₄ cup) caster
   (superfine) sugar, for sprinkling
Zest of 1 lemon

For the frosting

175 g (6 oz/³/₄ cup) cream cheese
100 g (3¹/₂ oz) icing
   (confectioners') sugar
Juice of half a lemon
Grated lemon zest, for sprinkling

Equipment

Stand mixer
Baking tray
Baking paper

Prep time: 20 minutes
First resting time: 1–2 hours
Shaping/proving time: 40 minutes
Baking time: 25 minutes

For the dough

Put the flour, salt, yeast, sugar, butter and egg in the bowl of a stand mixer fitted with a dough hook, keeping the salt and yeast apart. Pour in the milk and start mixing while pouring in the water. After 2 minutes, add the poppy seeds and continue to mix until it has come together into a smooth dough. Continue kneading in the stand mixer for 5 minutes (or if kneading by hand, knead for about 10 minutes) until elastic (see figure 1). Place the dough in an oiled bowl, cover with plastic wrap and leave to rise for 1–2 hours (see figure 2). Knock the air out of the dough and roll it out on a lightly floured worktop into a large rectangle.

For the filling

Brush over some softened butter, then sprinkle over some caster sugar. Grate the zest of a lemon over the top, being sure to cover the whole area lightly (see figure 3). Roll from the shortest side across, then cut into 8 thick slices. Place on a lined baking tray leaving a 4 cm (1¹/₂ inch) gap between each bun (see figure 4). Leave the buns to rest, covered loosely in oiled plastic wrap, for 40 minutes or until doubled in size. Preheat the oven to 180°C/350°F. Bake the buns for 25 minutes until golden. Leave to cool.

For the frosting

Mix the frosting ingredients together in a bowl until smooth but runny. Pour over the buns, then grate some lemon zest on top. Best if eaten on the day, but will keep in an airtight container for 1–2 days.

1. Knead the dough by hand or in a stand mixer until elastic.

2. Leave the dough to rise in an oiled bowl.

3. Sprinkle the rolled-out dough with caster sugar and grated lemon zest.

4. Place the cut buns on a lined baking tray and leave to prove until doubled in size.

BRIOCHE À TÊTE

Brioche is soft and sweet and goes well with both sweet and savoury dishes. The dough is very wet and hard to work with though, so I made it in a mixer and left it in a covered bowl in the fridge overnight to firm the butter up, which makes it easier to shape.

Brioche tête

Makes 10   Difficulty rating 🧤🧤

500 g (1 lb 2 oz/3¹/₃ cups)
   strong white flour, plus
   extra for dusting
7 g (2 teaspoons) fast-action
   dried yeast
50 g (1³/₄ oz) caster
   (superfine) sugar
1 teaspoon salt
140 ml (4³/₄ fl oz) milk
5 eggs
250 g (9 oz) butter, cut into
   small chunks
Zest of 1 orange or lemon
   (optional)
1 beaten egg mixed with
   a little milk, to brush

Equipment
Stand mixer
10 individual brioche moulds

Prep and chilling time: 15 minutes, plus at least 7 hours
Rising time: 2–3 hours
Baking time: 15–20 minutes

Put the flour in the bowl of the stand mixer fitted with the dough hook. Add the yeast, sugar and salt, making sure the salt and yeast do not come into contact. Warm the milk slightly (don't heat it too high or you will scald the yeast, stopping it from rising). Add the milk and eggs and mix for 2 minutes on a low speed. Stop the mixer and scrape down the sides. Add the butter, turn the speed up to medium-high and mix for 6–8 minutes until it comes together into a smooth dough.

Put the dough in a large greased bowl, cover with oiled plastic wrap and put it in the fridge for at least 7 hours, preferably overnight, to make the butter harden so that the dough can be shaped (see figure 1). Lightly dust a clean worktop with flour. Tip out the dough and knead for a few minutes to knock the air out (it is very wet still and will need a bit of working). Add the grated lemon or orange zest, if using, and knead until mixed.

Prepare each mould or tin by greasing it lightly. Break up the chilled dough into 10 large and 10 small pieces, and then roll into 10 large balls and 10 small balls (see figure 2). Place a small ball on top of each larger ball (see figure 3) and transfer to the mould or tin. Cover the moulds or tins and leave for 2–3 hours, or until the dough has doubled in size. Preheat the oven to 190°C/375°F. Brush the brioche with egg wash and bake for 15–20 minutes or until golden brown. These are best eaten the same day, but will keep in an airtight container for 2 days.

1. The brioche dough will be very stretchy after it has been proved.

2. Break up the dough into 20 balls; 10 slightly smaller than the rest.

3. Roll into balls and then top each larger ball with a smaller ball.

4. Brush the brioche dough with egg wash before baking.

STRAWBERRY LIME BRIOCHE BUNS

I had a punnet of strawberries I needed to use up, so I decided to make these brioche buns. They were so soft and pillowy and the lime icing went really well.

Strawberry lime brioche buns

Makes 8   Difficulty rating

For the brioche
500 g (1 lb 2 oz/3^1/$_3$ cups)
    strong white flour
110 g (3^3/$_4$ oz/^{1}/$_2$ cup)
    caster sugar
1^1/$_2$ teaspoons salt
7 g (2 teaspoons) fast-action
    dried yeast
3 large eggs
100 ml (3^1/$_2$ fl oz) milk
200 ml (7 fl oz/^{3}/$_4$ cups) water
110 g (3^3/$_4$ oz/^{1}/$_2$ cup)
    unsalted butter

For the flavouring
300 g (10 ^{1}/$_2$ oz) strawberries
60 g (2 oz/^{1}/$_4$ cup) caster sugar

For the icing
Juice and zest of 1 lime
50 g (1 ^{3}/$_4$ oz) icing
    (confectioners') sugar

Equipment
Stand mixer
Food processor
Baking tray
Baking paper

Prep time: 2 hours
Proving time: 40 minutes
Baking time: 25 minutes

For the brioche
Put the flour, sugar, salt and yeast in the bowl of a stand mixer fitted with a dough hook, making sure the yeast and salt do not come into contact. Add the eggs and milk and begin mixing while slowly pouring in the water. After 2 minutes, add the butter a tablespoon at a time. Continue mixing until combined, turn up the speed, then knead for 5 minutes. Place the dough in an oiled bowl and chill in the fridge for 2 hours or overnight.

For the flavouring and rolling
Put the strawberries in a food processor and blend so that you have about 200 ml (7 fl oz/^{3}/$_4$ cups) purée. Transfer the purée to a pan and add the sugar. Stir over a low heat and let the strawberries cook and reduce for 10 minutes until thick (see figure 1). Press the purée through a sieve, then leave to cool.

Dust a worktop with flour and tip out the risen dough. Roll out to a large rectangle and spread the strawberry mixture all over in an even layer (see figure 2). Fold the dough in half and slice across the width into 5 cm (2 inch) strips (see figure 3). Twist and wrap each strip around your hand to make a bun shape (see figure 4). Place on a lined baking tray and leave to rise for 40 minutes. Preheat the oven to 180°C/350°F. Bake the buns for 20–25 minutes until golden.

To make the icing, add some lime juice to the icing sugar in a bowl and mix. Drizzle it over each bun and sprinkle with some lime zest. These are best eaten the same day, but will keep in an airtight container for 2 days.

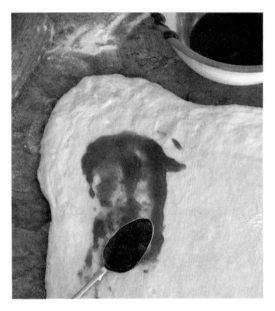

1. Cook your strawberry purée until it has reduced and thickened.

2. Spread the purée over the top of the rolled-out dough.

3. Fold the dough in half and cut into long thin strips.

4. Twist and wrap the strips of dough around your fingers to make a bun shape.

CINNAMON DANISH PASTRY SWIRLS

My partner and I often buy cinnamon Danish pastries from the bakery, so I decided to try making my own and I'm so glad I did, because they are amazing. The dough takes a little time to make but the process is not difficult; it just requires a lot of folding and resting time, so I would suggest making the dough the evening before you need it. My partner asked for a lemon drizzle icing, which made these delicious pastries taste even better.

Cinnamon Danish pastry swirls

Makes 10   Difficulty rating 🧤🧤

For the dough

250 g (9 oz/1²/₃ cups) strong
   white flour
40 g (1¹/₂ oz) caster
   (superfine) sugar
1 teaspoon salt
7 g (2 teaspoons) fast-action
   dried yeast
1 egg
45 ml (1¹/₂ fl oz) tepid water
65 ml (2 fl oz/¹/₄ cup) milk
250 g (9 oz/1 cup)
   unsalted butter

For the filling

175 g (6 oz) unsalted butter
60 g (2 oz/¹/₂ cup) soft light
   brown sugar
3 teaspoons ground cinnamon
2 teaspoons icing
   (confectioners') sugar
1 egg, beaten

For the lemon drizzle

2 tablespoons lemon juice
1 teaspoon grated lemon zest
75 g (2³/₄ oz) icing
   (confectioners') sugar

continued overleaf ...

Prep time: 30 minutes
Resting time: 8 plus 1¹/₂ hours or overnight
Proving time: 2 hours
Baking time: 15–20 minutes

For the dough

Put the flour, sugar, salt and yeast in the bowl of a stand mixer fitted with a dough hook, making sure the salt and yeast don't come into contact. Start mixing, while you add the egg, water and milk. Knead the dough for about 6 minutes. Lightly dust a worktop with flour and tip the dough out. Roll the dough into a ball and place it in a clean, dry plastic bag in the fridge while you prepare the butter.

Place the butter between 2 sheets of baking paper. Hit it with a rolling pin to flatten it into a rectangle (see figure 1).

Take the dough out of the fridge and roll it out on the floured surface into a large rectangle. Place the flattened butter in the middle (see figure 2) and fold the dough over it (see figure 3). Turn it, then roll the dough out to a large rectangle again. Fold in half again, then follow these folding and rolling steps twice more. Cover the dough with plastic wrap and return to the fridge for 1 hour.

Once rested, roll out the dough and fold, turn and roll twice more. Return the dough to the fridge for 30 minutes. Remove from the fridge, roll out the dough and fold again, twice, then leave the dough to rest in the fridge for at least 8 hours or overnight (see figure 4).

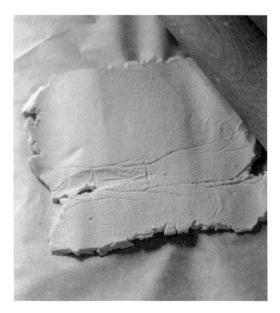

1. Roll the block of butter between 2 sheets of baking paper.

2. Place the butter on top of the rolled dough.

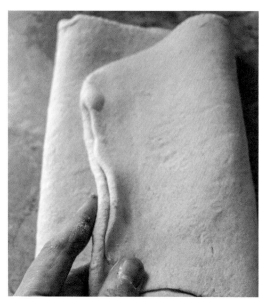

3. Roll, fold, turn and roll again as instructed.

4. Fold and rest in the fridge for at least 8 hours or overnight.

Equipment
Stand mixer
Clean plastic bag
Rolling pin
Plastic wrap
Baking paper
Baking tray

For the filling
Melt the butter in a small saucepan over a gentle heat just until it's thick but not too runny. Add the sugar, cinnamon and icing sugar and mix it all together (see figure 5).

Roll out the dough on a floured surface into a large rectangle and spread over the filling. Roll each side of the rectangle in to meet in the middle (see figures 6 and 7), then cut into 5 cm (2 inch) thick slices. Place the cut slices on a lined baking tray with space in between (see figure 8) and leave to prove for 2 hours, or until doubled in size.

Preheat the oven to 200°C/400°F. Brush some beaten egg on top of each pastry and bake for 15–20 minutes.

For the lemon drizzle
Mix the lemon juice, lemon zest and icing sugar in a bowl to form a nice runny icing, then drizzle it over the baked pastries.

These are best eaten the same day, but will keep in an airtight container for 2 days.

5. Melt the butter and mix the filling ingredients together in a small pan.

6. Spread the filling over the surface of the rolled-out dough in an even layer.

7. Roll the dough up from each side to meet in the middle.

8. Cut the rolled dough into slices and place on a lined baking tray.

SWEET APPLE CINNAMON PRETZELS

My mum visited an apple orchard near where we live
and came back with loads of apples. She dropped off
a bag for me too, so I thought it would be nice to make
a sweet pretzel with apple purée in the dough and
a cinnamon sugar coating.

Sweet apple cinnamon pretzels

Makes 8–12   Difficulty rating

For the dough

350 g (12 oz/2¹/₃ cups) plain
    (all-purpose) flour, plus extra
    for dusting
200 g (7 oz/1¹/₃ cups) strong
    white flour (bread flour)
1 teaspoon salt
40 g (1¹/₂ oz) unsalted butter
250 ml (9 oz/1 cup) apple purée
    (2 or 3 apples, peeled, cored
    and puréed in a blender)
3 tablespoons caster
    (superfine) sugar
7 g (2 teaspoons) fast-action
    dried yeast
300 ml (10¹/₂ fl oz/1¹/₄ cup)
    warm water

For the cooking and topping

500 ml (17 fl oz/2 cups) water
3 tablespoons baking powder
2–3 tablespoons ground
    cinnamon
60 g (2 oz/¹/₂ cup)
    demerara sugar

Equipment

Oiled baking tray
Pan

Prep time: 30 minutes
Resting time: 1 hour
Baking time: 20–25 minutes

For the dough

Put the flours, salt, butter and apple purée in a large bowl and
rub it all together until it resembles breadcrumbs. Add the
sugar and yeast, then pour over half the water. Mix with your
hands until it starts to come together, then add the rest and
continue to mix until it comes together into a smooth dough.

Lightly dust a clean worktop with flour and tip the dough out.
Knead for 5 minutes until smooth. Put the dough in an oiled
bowl, cover with plastic wrap and leave to rise for 1 hour.

Tip the dough out onto the floured worktop and knock out the
air. Divide the dough into 12 small or 8 larger, even-sized balls
and roll out each piece into a long rope. Fold the ropes into a
pretzel shape and place on an oiled tray (see figures 1 to 4).
Preheat the oven to 180°C/350°F.

For the cooking and topping

Put the water and baking powder in a saucepan and bring
to the boil. Gently lower in the pretzels, poaching one at a
time for 1 minute each. Place the poached pretzels back on the
baking tray.

Mix the cinnamon and sugar together in a small bowl. Brush
the pretzels with beaten egg, then sprinkle over the cinnamon
sugar. Bake for 20–25 minutes until golden. These are best eaten
the same day, but will keep in an airtight container for 2 days.

1. Start off with the rope in a 'U' shape and then cross the two ends over.

2. Continue to twist together a couple of times, leaving the ends free.

3. Bring the ends up towards the top of the circle and lay the ends over the edge.

4. The finished pretzel shape..

Pumpkin pecan cinnamon buns

Makes 10   Difficulty rating

For the dough
500 g (1 lb 2 oz/3$^1/_3$ cups)
strong white flour
110 g (3$^3/_4$ oz/$^1/_2$ cup) caster
(superfine) sugar
1$^1/_2$ teaspoons salt
7 g (2 teaspoons) fast-action
dried yeast
2 large eggs
120 g (4$^1/_2$ oz/$^1/_2$ cup)
pumpkin purée
60 ml (2 fl oz/$^1/_4$ cup) milk
120 ml (4 fl oz/$^1/_2$ cup) water
60 g (2 oz/$^1/_2$ cup) unsalted
butter

For the filling
70 g (1$^1/_2$ oz/$^1/_2$ cup) pecans
100 g (3$^1/_2$ oz/$^1/_3$ cup) golden
syrup or maple syrup
100 g (3$^1/_2$ oz/$^1/_2$ cup) soft light
brown sugar
60 g (2 oz/$^1/_4$ cup) butter, melted
1 teaspoon ground cinnamon

For the topping
50 g (1$^3/_4$ oz) icing
(confectioners') sugar
1 tablespoon maple syrup

Equipment
Stand mixer
Oiled bowl
Food processor
Baking tray

Prep time: 20 minutes
First rising time: 1–2 hours
Second rising time: 30 minutes
Baking time: 20–25 minutes

For the dough
Put the flour, sugar, salt and yeast in the bowl of a stand mixer fitted with a dough hook, making sure the yeast and salt do not come into contact. Add the eggs, pumpkin purée and milk and mix together. Slowly pour in the water as it kneads and mix for 2 minutes. Add the butter a tablespoon at a time and continue kneading until combined. Turn up the speed and knead for 5 minutes. Place the dough into an oiled bowl and leave to rise for 1–2 hours.

For the filling
Put the pecans in a food processor and chop until fine. Mix the chopped nuts with the golden syrup, sugar, melted butter and cinnamon in a bowl.

Once the dough has risen, roll it out on a lightly floured surface into a large rectangle. Spread the mixture on top in an even layer. Roll up the dough into a log and then cut into 5 cm (2 inch) slices and lay on a lined baking tray, leaving a gap between each one. Leave to prove for about 30 minutes.

Preheat the oven to 180°C/350°F. Bake for 20–25 minutes until golden brown.

For the topping
Mix the icing sugar with the maple syrup, then drizzle over the buns. These are best eaten the same day, but will keep in an airtight container for 2 days.

Giant pecan pie Chelsea bun

Makes 1 large bun / serves 8   Difficulty rating 🧤

For the dough

500 g (1 lb 2 oz/3¹/₃ cups) strong
   white flour, plus extra to dust
¹/₂ teaspoon salt
7 g (2 teaspoons) fast-action
   dried yeast
40 g (1¹/₂ oz) caster
   (superfine) sugar
40 g (1¹/₂ oz) unsalted
   butter, softened
1 egg, beaten
100 ml (3¹/₂ fl oz/¹/₃ cup plus
   1 tablespoon) milk
200 ml (7 fl oz/³/₄ cup) warm water

For the filling

70 g (2¹/₂ oz) pecans
95 g (3¹/₄ oz/¹/₃ cup) butter, melted
160 g (5³/₄ oz) soft light
   brown sugar
3 tablespoons golden syrup

For the drizzle

2 tablespoons caramel sauce
50 g (1³/₄ oz) icing
   (confectioners') sugar

Equipment

Stand mixer
Oiled bowl
Food processor
Greased 30 cm (12 inch)
   baking tin

Prep time: 20 minutes
First rising time: 1–2 hours
Second rising time: 40 minutes
Baking time: 20–25 minutes

For the dough

Put the flour, salt, yeast, sugar, butter and egg into the bowl of a stand mixer fitted with a dough hook, making sure the salt and yeast do not come into contact. Pour in the milk, then start mixing with the dough hook while pouring in the water. Continue to mix until it comes together. Knead for 6 minutes in the mixer (or about 10 minutes if kneading by hand) until elastic. Place in an oiled bowl, cover with plastic wrap and leave to rise for 1–2 hours.

For the filling and assembly

Put the pecans in a food processor and chop until fine. Melt the butter in a small pan over a gentle heat. Add the sugar and syrup and stir to combine. Add the pecans and stir through.

Lightly dust a clean worktop with flour and roll out the dough into a long rectangle. Spread the filling all over in an even layer. Slice into long 5 cm (2 inch) strips. Roll into a spiral, starting with one strip and rolling straight into the next strip, until all the strips have been used, to make one giant rolled bun. Place the bun in the greased baking tin and leave for 40 minutes, or until doubled in size. Preheat the oven to 200°C/400°F. Bake for 20–25 minutes until golden.

For the drizzle

Mix the caramel sauce with the icing sugar in a bowl, then drizzle over the giant bun and enjoy. This is best eaten the same day, but will keep in an airtight container for 2 days.

RHUBARB CRUMBLE AND CUSTARD MACARONS

I made a roasted rhubarb curd for these, then added some custard powder to the buttercream and rolled them in some crumble. Homemade macarons just seem to taste a lot better than any I have tried from the shops. They are a bit fiddly to make and the kitchen always looks such a mess afterwards, but they are always worth it.

Rhubarb crumble and custard macarons

Makes 20 Difficulty rating 🧤🧤🧤

For the macaron shell

110 g (3³/₄ oz/1²/₃ cups)
  ground almonds
200 g (7 oz) icing
  (confectioners') sugar
100 g (3¹/₂ oz) egg whites
¹/₂ teaspoon salt
50 g (1³/₄ oz) caster
  (superfine) sugar
Gel peach food colouring
  (optional) – I dip a skewer
  into the pot of colouring,
  then dip it into the mixture
Pink gel food colouring

For the rhubarb curd

3–4 rhubarb stalks, chopped
110 g (3³/₄ oz/¹/₂ cup)
  caster sugar
3 egg yolks
80 g (2³/₄ oz) unsalted butter

continued overleaf ...

Prep time: 40 minutes
Resting time: 20–60 minutes
Baking time: 50 minutes

For the macaron shell

Put the ground almonds in a food processor and pulse until fine. Add the icing sugar and pulse again until a fine powder.

Whip the egg whites and salt in a clean bowl until foamy and add the caster sugar a spoonful at a time. Whip until the mixture reaches stiff peaks. Add a little peach colouring at this point, if you are using (see figure 1).

Sift in one-quarter of the almond/sugar mixture and fold it together (see figure 2). Add the next quarter and continue folding in until it is combined (see figure 3). Try not to over-work it. Add the rest of the almond/sugar mix.

Put one half of the mixture into a piping bag fitted with a round 1 cm (¹/₂ inch) nozzle. Add pink colouring to the half left in the bowl, then put this in a separate piping bag (see figure 4). Pipe a big blob of each onto a circle on a macaron mat (see figure 5), then use a toothpick to blend the colours and swirl them around to create a marble effect (see figure 6).

Leave the macarons to sit to form a skin. I find that the time required varies depending on the weather, so keep an eye on them – it can take from about 20 minutes to an hour.

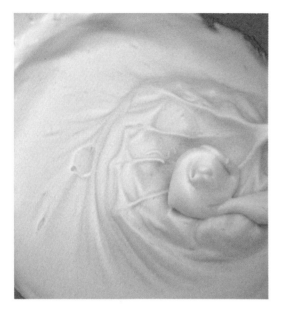

1. Whip the egg whites to stiff peaks and add a little peach colouring.

2. Sift in one-quarter of the almond and sugar mixture and fold together.

3. Add the next quarter and continue folding until mixed.

4. Spoon the two different coloured mixtures into separate piping bags.

5. Pipe a circle of each colour onto the macaron mat.

6. Use a toothpick to swirl the two colours together for each macaron.

7. Pipe buttercream around half the macarons and put some rhubarb curd in the centre.

8. Roll the sides of the macarons in the crumble mixture.

For the crumble

110 g (3³/₄ oz/³/₄ cup) plain
   (all-purpose) flour
60 g (2 oz/¹/₄ cup) granulated
   (white) sugar
Pinch of salt
4 tablespoons unsalted
   butter, melted

For the buttercream

110 g (3³/₄ oz/¹/₂ cup)
   unsalted butter
100 g (3¹/₂ oz/1 cup) icing
   (confectioners') sugar
3 tablespoons custard powder
1 teaspoon vanilla extract

Equipment

Food processor
Piping bags
Macaron baking mat
Baking tray

Preheat the oven to 140°C/275°F. Bake the macarons for 20 minutes until risen and the top of the macaron has a hard shell. Leave them to rest for 5 minutes and then gently remove them from the mat ready to be filled.

For the rhubarb curd and crumble

Preheat the oven to 180°C/350°F.

First make the rhubarb curd. Put the rhubarb on a baking tray, sprinkle over the sugar and bake for 20 minutes or until soft. Transfer to a food processor and purée. Press through a sieve into a pan, add the yolks and sugar and mix. Stir continuously over a low heat until it thickens and coats the back of the spoon. Pour into a bowl, stir in the butter and leave to cool.

Now, make the crumble. Combine the flour, sugar and a pinch of salt in a small bowl. Add the melted butter and mix until the dry ingredients are moistened and the mixture comes together in large clumps. Spread out on a baking tray and bake in the oven for 5 minutes. Take it out of the oven, stir it around a bit and then return to the oven for a further 5 minutes.

For the buttercream and assembly

Put the butter in a mixing bowl, add the icing sugar, custard powder and vanilla extract and mix until smooth. Spoon into a piping bag and pipe around the edge of half the macarons (piping on the flat side).

Spoon a little rhubarb curd into the centre of each buttercream swirl and top with a macaron shell (see figure 7). Roll the macarons in the crumble so it sticks to the buttercream around the edge (see figure 8). These will keep in the fridge for 1 week.

PERSONAL APPLE PIE

Sometimes its nice to just have a pie all to yourself and
I hate making a big pie just for the two of us. I baked this
pie in a large tea cup. It could be shared with two spoons
if you don't want to eat it all. There is enough dough to
make one large mug pie or two smaller ones. I also made two
leaves with the offcuts of dough and stuck them on top,
but you could decorate them any way you like.

Personal apple pie

Makes 1   Difficulty rating

30 g (1 oz) unsalted
    butter, chilled
50 g (1³/₄ oz/¹/₃ cup) plain
    (all-purpose) flour
1 large apple
30 g (1 oz) caster
    (superfine) sugar
Milk, for brushing

Equipment
1 large tea cup

Prep time: 10 minutes
Resting time: 10 minutes
Baking time: 20 minutes

Rub the butter and flour together in a mixing bowl until it resembles breadcrumbs (see figure 1). Add 1 teaspoon of water and bring the mixture together into a ball (see figure 2). Leave the dough to rest for 10 minutes while you preheat the oven to 180°C/350°F.

Peel the apple, cut it into chunks and put in a bowl. Add the sugar and mix so the all apple is evenly coated.

Take a small piece of the pastry and roll into a long strip. Place the strip around the lip of the cup and then fill the cup with the apples (see figure 3).

Roll out the rest of the dough on a lightly floured surface into a circle large enough to cover the top of the cup. Place the pastry on top of the cup and press onto the rim of pastry.

Brush the top with milk and make a slit for air to escape (see figure 4). Bake for 20 minutes until golden.

1. Rub the butter and flour together.

2. Bring the mixture together into a ball.

3. Fit a strip of pastry around the rim of the tea cup and fill the cup with the apple.

4. Brush the top of the pie with a little milk before baking.

Banoffee brioche loaf

Makes 1 large loaf or 2 small loaves   Difficulty rating 🧤🧤

For the dough

500 g (1 lb 2 oz/3^1/$_3$ cups)
  strong white flour
60 g (2 oz/^{1}/$_3$ cup) soft light
  brown sugar
1^1/$_2$ teaspoons salt
2^1/$_2$ teaspoons fast-action
  dried yeast
3 large eggs
100 ml (3^1/$_2$ fl oz) milk
3 tablespoons dulce de leche
200 ml (7 fl oz/^{3}/$_4$ cups) water
110 g (3^3/$_4$ oz) unsalted butter

For the filling

60 g (2 oz/^{1}/$_4$ cup)
  unsalted butter
60 g (2 oz/^{1}/$_3$ cup) soft light
  brown sugar
2 bananas, peeled and sliced
4 tablespoons dulce de leche

Equipment

Stand mixer
Oiled bowl
Loaf tin

Prep time: 10 minutes
Rising time: 2 hours
Proving and shaping time: 1 hour
Baking time: 30 minutes

Put the flour, sugar, salt and yeast into the bowl of a stand mixer fitted with a dough hook, making sure the salt and yeast do not come into contact. Add the eggs, milk and dulce de leche and slowly pour in the water as you mix for 2 minutes. Add the butter a tablespoon at a time and continue mixing until combined. Turn up the speed and knead for 5 minutes. Put the dough in an oiled bowl and leave to rise for 1–2 hours.

For the filling

Lightly dust a clean worktop with flour and roll the dough out into a long thin rectangle.

Melt the butter and brush on top of the rolled out dough. Sprinkle over the sugar and add slices of banana so that the surface is covered. Drizzle over the dulce de leche and roll the sheet up from the long side into a log shape. Slice in half and twist the 2 strips together. Place in the loaf tin and leave to prove for 40 minutes.

Preheat the oven to 180°C/350°F. Bake the loaf for 30 minutes until the it sounds hollow when tapped.

This is best eaten the same day, but will keep in an airtight container for 2 days.

PINEAPPLE ORANGE PAVLOVA

Pineapple flowers are so impressive — I think they look like sunflowers! I decided to use them for this tiered pavlova. I used the leftover pineapple and egg yolks to make a curd to go in it and added orange and lemon — it was so refreshing.

When I make meringues, I always weigh the egg whites and use double that weight for the sugar.

Pineapple orange pavlova

Makes one 3-tiered pavlova   Difficulty rating 🧤🧤

For the pineapple flowers
1 pineapple

For the meringue
180 g (6 oz) egg whites
    (about 4–5 eggs – keep
    the yolks for the curd)
360 g (12³/₄ oz) caster
    (superfine) sugar

For the curd
60 g (2 oz) caster
    (superfine) sugar
Juice and zest of 1 orange
Juice of ¹/₄ pineapple
Juice and zest of 1 lemon
4 egg yolks
80 g (2³/₄ oz) unsalted butter
600 ml (21 fl oz) thick (double/
    heavy) cream
2 tablespoons icing sugar
2 oranges, segmented

continued overleaf ...

Prep time: 20 minutes
Bake time for pineapple flowers: 1¹/₂ hours
Prep time for meringue: 20 minutes
Baking time: 1 and half hours
Curd/decoration time: 30 minutes

For the pineapple flowers
Make these dainty flowers at the same time as the meringue.
Preheat the oven to 100°C/200°F.

Cut the peel from the pineapple, then slice into thin pieces
using a mandolin (see figure 1). Lay the slices on a lined baking
tray (see figure 2) and bake for 1 hour. Remove from the oven
and turn each flower over.

Bake for another 30–60 minutes or until they have dried out.
Place each flower in the hole of a muffin tin to shape the edges
(see figure 3).

For the meringue
Preheat the oven to 180°C/350°F.

Put the sugar on a baking tray and place in the oven for
5 minutes to heat up. Begin whisking the egg whites in a stand
mixer, then pour in the warmed sugar.

Turn the oven down to 100°C/200°F – leave the door open for
5 minutes to cool the oven so you don't scald the meringues.

Continue mixing for 5–8 minutes until the egg whites have
tripled in volume and are shiny. Spoon the meringue mixture
into a piping bag. Pipe 4 circles in different sizes going from
large to small on a lined baking tray (see figure 4).

1. Slice the pineapple on a mandolin.

2. Arrange the pineapple slices on a lined baking tray.

3. Bake the flowers until dried out and cool in the holes of a muffin tin.

4. Pipe meringue nests of different sizes on a lined baking tray.

Equipment

Mandolin
Baking tray
Baking paper
Muffin tin
Stand mixer
Piping bag

Build up into nest shapes by piping around the edges. Bake for 1 hour. Remove from the oven and carefully remove the smallest meringue. Continue baking the rest for another 30 minutes. Check them at this point – if they are still soft on the base, continue for another 30 minutes, checking regularly.

For the curd

Put the egg yolks, sugar, juice and zests in a saucepan and stir. Heat over a medium heat, stirring constantly, until the mixture starts to thicken. Once it coats the back of a spoon, remove the pan from the heat and pour it into a bowl. Stir in the butter and leave to cool.

Whip the cream with 2 tablespoons icing sugar until thick. Spoon the cream onto each layer of meringue nest and drizzle in some curd and add some orange slices.

Build the filled nests into a tower, adding cream, curd and orange segments to each layer (see figures 5 to 7). Use cream to attach the pineapple flowers all around the stacked pavlova (see figure 8).

5. Place the largest meringue nest on a serving plate and fill with cream, a drizzle of curd and some orange segments.

6. Top with the next size meringue nest and fill as before.

7. Continue to layer the meringues and finish with the smallest nest, some cream and a drizzle of curd.

8. Attach the dried pineapple flowers all around the pavlova using the cream to help them stay in position.

3. Savoury bakes

QUAIL'S EGG-STUFFED PORK PIES

Pork pies are an English tradition, but I have livened these ones up with a quail's eggs in the middle. It was really nice to have a go at making my own because I could experiment with the sizes. I found I preferred these small ones to a larger single pie or the tiny picnic-sized ones.

Quail's egg-stuffed pork pies

Makes 6   Difficulty rating 🧤🧤

For the eggs
6 quail's eggs

For the pastry
200 g (7 oz/1¹/₃ cups) plain
   (all-purpose) flour
40 g (1¹/₂ oz) strong white flour
60 g (2 oz/¹/₄ cup)
   unsalted butter
100 ml (3¹/₂ fl oz) water
1 teaspoons salt
60 g (2 oz/¹/₄ cup) lard

For the filling
1 onion, finely chopped
400 g (14 oz) minced
   (ground) pork
1 teaspoon English mustard
¹/₂ teaspoon wholegrain mustard
Pinch of nutmeg
Salt and freshly ground
   black pepper
1 chicken stock cube
2 gelatine leaves
150 ml (5 fl oz) boiling water

Equipment
Rolling pin
6-hole muffin tin, greased,
   with strips of baking paper
   in each hole

Prep time: 25 minutes
Baking time: 40 minutes, plus overnight setting

For the eggs
First boil the quail's eggs in a pan of boiling water for 2 minutes. Drain and rinse under cold water, then peel. Set aside.

For the pastry
Preheat the oven to 200°C/400°F. Put the flours and butter in a bowl and rub together until the mixture resembles breadcrumbs. Put the water in a pan with the salt and lard and boil until the lard melts. Pour into the bowl with the flour and butter. Mix until a ball of dough forms. Lightly dust a clean worktop with flour and tip the dough out. Roll out to 1 cm (½ inch) thick, then cut large circles with a pastry cutter so that they are just larger than the holes in your tin. Press the circles into the holes of the tin, leaving a little pastry overhanging (see figure 1). Save the rest of the pastry for the lids.

For the filling
Mix the onion, pork, mustards, nutmeg and salt and pepper in a bowl. Put a little of the mixture into each pastry case (see figure 2). Add a boiled egg to the centre of each (see figure 3), then add more meat around the eggs so they are covered. Roll out the rest of the dough on the floured worktop and cut circles for the lids. Top each pie with a pastry circle and press to attach to the rim of pastry (see figure 4). Make small holes in the middle of each lid to let air escape during baking. Bake for 40 minutes until golden. Remove from the oven and leave to cool in the tin.

Dissolve the stock cube and gelatine in the boiling water. Pour the stock into the holes in the lids, then leave in the fridge overnight to set. Store in the fridge. They are best eaten within 2–3 days.

1. Gently press the pastry circles into the prepared tin.

2. Put a little meat mixture in the base of each pastry case.

3. Add a boiled egg and then top with more meat so that the egg is covered.

4. Top each pie with a pastry lid and press to attach it to the rim.

Spicy tomato macarons

Makes 12   Difficulty rating 🧤🧤

For the macarons

175 g (6 oz) egg whites, separated

210 g (7^1/$_2$ oz) icing
   (confectioners') sugar

210 g (7^1/$_2$ oz) ground almonds

3 tablespoons tomato powder,
   plus more for sprinkling

1 teaspoon paprika

^{1}/$_2$ teaspoon chilli powder

^{1}/$_4$ teaspoon freshly ground
   black pepper

165 ml (5^1/$_4$ fl oz) water

235 g (8^1/$_2$ oz) granulated
   (white) sugar

Dried oregano, for sprinkling

For the filling

210 g (7^1/$_2$ oz/1 cup) cream cheese

2 tablespoons tomato purée

1 teaspoon paprika

2 tablespoons chopped chives

^{1}/$_4$ teaspoon freshly ground
   black pepper

Equipment

Stand mixer

Sugar thermometer

Piping bag fitted with a 1 cm
   (^{1}/$_2$ inch) nozzle (tip)

Baking tray

Baking paper

Piping bag

Prep time: 30 minutes

Baking time: 10 minutes

For the macarons

Weigh the eggs so that you have 80 g (2^3/$_4$ oz) in one bowl and
90 g (3^1/$_4$ oz) in another. Put the larger amount of whites in the
bowl of a stand mixer fitted with the whisk attachment. Sift the
icing sugar, ground almonds, tomato powder, paprika, chilli
powder and pepper into a large bowl. Stir in the smaller amount
of whites to make a paste. Preheat the oven to 180°C/350°F.

Put the water and granulated sugar in a pan and heat over a
medium heat. When it gets to about 110°C (230°F) add a pinch
of sugar to the egg whites in the stand mixer and whip until
peaks form. Turn the mixer down to low until the sugar syrup is
ready. As soon as it reaches 120°C (250°F), turn the mixer up to
high speed and pour the hot syrup slowly down the side of the
bowl. Whip until thick and glossy. Fold one-third of the mixture
into the almond mixture, then add the rest a bit at a time, folding
as you go. Spoon this into the piping bag.

Line baking trays with baking paper and pipe the macarons
in small circles. Tap the tray onto the worktop to remove any
air bubbles. Sprinkle over some tomato powder and oregano
and set aside to form a skin on top. Turn the oven down to
120°C/325°F and bake the macarons for about 10 minutes.
Leave them to cool on the tray for 5 minutes before removing
them gently and placing them on a wire cooling rack.

For the filling

Mix all the ingredients together in a bowl, then spoon into a
piping bag. Pipe a swirl of filling onto the flat side of half the
macarons, then sandwich with the rest.

Sour cream, cheddar and chive drop scones

Makes 12   Difficulty rating

250 g (9 oz/1²/3 cups) plain
  (all-purpose) flour
50 g (1¹/2 oz/¹/2 cup) cheddar
  cheese, grated, plus a little
  extra for sprinkling
¹/2 teaspoon salt
¹/2 teaspoon freshly ground
  black pepper
2 teaspoons baking powder
1 teaspoon bicarbonate of soda
  (baking soda)
1 teaspoon soft light
  brown sugar
60 g (2 oz/¹/4 cup) butter
40 g (1¹/2 oz/¹/3 cup)
  chives, chopped
¹/2 teaspoon English or
  wholegrain mustard
250 ml (9 fl oz/1 cup) buttermilk
120 ml (4 fl oz/¹/2 cup)
  sour cream

Equipment
Baking trays
Baking paper
Ice-cream scoop or large spoon

Prep time: 10 minutes
Baking time: 12–15 minutes

Preheat the oven to 220°C/425°F and line 2 baking trays with baking paper.

Put the flour, cheese, salt, pepper, baking powder, bicarbonate of soda and sugar in a bowl. Rub in the butter with your fingers until it resembles breadcrumbs.

Add the chives and mix through. Add the mustard, buttermilk and sour cream and mix until it all comes together.

Use an ice-cream scoop or a large spoon to spoon mounds of the scone mixture onto the prepared baking trays leaving a 5 cm (2 inch) gap between each one to allow room for them to spread.

Sprinkle some more cheddar cheese on top and bake for about 12–15 minutes until golden and risen. These scones are best eaten the same day, but will keep for 3 days in an airtight container.

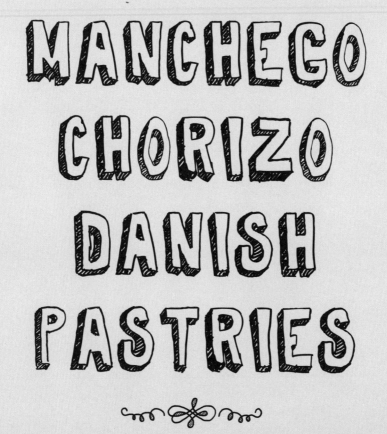

MANCHEGO CHORIZO DANISH PASTRIES

These savoury Danish pastries are a great treat and would be the perfect gift to take along to a brunch date. They take a while to make but are worth it.

Manchego chorizo Danish pastries

Makes 8   Difficulty rating 🧤🧤

For the pastry

250 g (9 oz/1²/₃ cups)
   strong white flour
1 teaspoon salt
7 g (2 teaspoons) fast-action
   dried yeast
1 egg, plus 1 for brushing
45 ml (1¹/₂ fl oz) tepid water
65 ml (2 fl oz/¹/₄ cup) milk
125 g (4¹/₂ oz/¹/₂ cup) butter
   (in one block)

For the filling

100 g (3¹/₂ oz/1 cup) Manchego
   cheese, thinly sliced
16 slices of chorizo
2 tablespoons smoked paprika

Equipment

Stand mixer
Rolling pin
Baking tray
Pastry brush

Prep time: 20 minutes
Rising time: 8 hours or overnight, plus 1 hour
Bake time: 25 minutes

For the pastry

Use the ingredients to make a dough in the stand mixer following the instructions on page 80. Lightly dust a clean worktop with flour and tip the dough out. Roll the dough into a ball and place it in a clean dry plastic bag in the fridge while you flatten the butter. Place the butter between 2 sheets of baking paper. Hit it with a rolling pin to flatten it into a rectangle.

Take the dough out of the fridge and roll it into a large rectangle. Place the flattened butter in the centre and continue to fold, turn, roll and rest as instructed on page 80. Leave the dough to rest in the fridge for at least 8 hours or overnight.

For the filling

Roll out the dough on a floured surface and cut it into triangles (see figure 1). Put 2 slices of cheese and 2 chorizo slices in the centre of each triangle and dust with some paprika (see figure 2).

Roll the pastry up into crescents, like a croissant (see figure 3), and place them on a lined baking tray. Loosely cover and leave them to rise for 1 hour. Preheat the oven to 180°C/350°F.

Brush the pastries with a beaten egg, and dust the tops with a little paprika (see figure 4). Bake for 25 minutes until golden.

1. Roll out the dough and cut into triangles.

2. Put 2 slices of cheese and 2 chorizo slices on each triangle and dust with paprika.

3. Roll the triangles into crescents starting at the wide end.

4. Dust the tops of the rolled pastries with some more paprika before baking.

Feta, Greek yoghurt and herb muffins with tomatoes

Makes 6   Difficulty rating 🧤

50 ml (1 1/2 fl oz) vegetable oil
1 egg
125 g (4 1/2 oz/1/2 cup)
    Greek yoghurt
125 g (4 1/2 oz) plain
    (all-purpose) flour
1 teaspoon salt
Freshly ground black pepper
3 tablespoons chopped
    fresh basil
1/2 teaspoon fresh thyme
1/2 teaspoon fresh
    chopped chives
1 garlic clove, grated
1 teaspoon baking powder
100 g (3 1/2 oz) feta cheese,
    broken into small pieces
6 cherry tomatoes

Equipment
Muffin cases
6-hole muffin tin
Greaseproof paper cut to size

Prep time: 10 minutes
Baking time: 15–20 minutes

Preheat the oven to 180°C/350°F. Line the muffin tin with the cases.

Put the oil and egg in a bowl with the Greek yoghurt and mix together. Add the flour, salt, a little pepper, herbs, garlic and baking powder and stir together.

Add the feta cheese and fold through the mixture until just mixed through. Be careful not to overmix.

Spoon the mixture evenly into the muffin cases and push a cherry tomato into each one.

Bake for about 15–20 minutes until golden and risen. These are best eaten the same day, but will keep in an airtight container for 2 days.

CHICKEN PIE CONES

I love chicken pie in all its forms. These unusual and quirky pies are going to be a huge hit with kids as they are made into puff pastry cones and look like a delicious savoury ice cream.

Chicken pie cones

Makes 6   Difficulty rating 🧤🧤

For the pastry

250 g (9 oz/1²/₃ cups) plain
 (all-purpose) flour
1 teaspoon salt
Juice of ¹/₄ lemon
100 ml (3¹/₂ fl oz) cold water
200 g (7 oz) unsalted
 butter (in one block)

For the filling

¹/₂ red onion, finely chopped
1 tablespoon soft light
 brown sugar
2 garlic cloves, crushed
200 g (7 oz/1 cup) bacon lardons
3 chicken breasts, chopped
 into small pieces
60 g (2 oz/¹/₄ cup) butter
2 tablespoons cornflour
250 ml (9 fl oz/1 cup) milk
250 ml (9 fl oz/1 cup) thick
 (double/heavy) cream
1 tablespoon English mustard
150 g (5¹/₂ oz) cheddar
 cheese, chopped
2 tablespoons smoked
 spreadable cheddar
¹/₄ teaspoon freshly ground
 black pepper
1 teaspoon chopped
 fresh tarragon

continued overleaf ...

Prep time: 50 minutes
Rising time: 1 hour 30 minutes
Baking time: 30 minutes

For the pastry

Put the flour and salt in a large bowl and add the lemon juice and water and knead together for a few minutes until smooth. Shape into a ball, make 2 cuts to create a cross and put the dough in a clean plastic bag in the fridge for 1 hour.

Place the block of butter between 2 pieces of baking paper and use a rolling pin to hit it evenly until it forms a thin square.

Remove the dough from the fridge and pull each corner made by the slits outwards to stretch the dough. Lightly dust a clean worktop with flour and roll the dough out into a large envelope shape.

Place the butter in the centre and fold the dough in to the centre to cover the butter. Press together and then roll the dough out into a large rectangle. Fold each end to the centre and then fold in half – this is a book fold.

Turn the dough 90 degrees clockwise and then roll out again into a rectangle. Fold one-quarter of one short side into the centre and then fold the rest over the top. Wrap the dough in plastic wrap and place in the fridge for 30 minutes.

Preheat the oven to 180°C/350°F. Roll out the dough on the floured worktop into a large rectangle and cut into 2.5 cm (1 inch) wide strips (see figure 1). Wrap the strips around the cream horn moulds and bake for 30 minutes until golden (see figures 2 to 4).

1. Roll the dough out and cut into 2.5 cm (1 inch) wide strips.

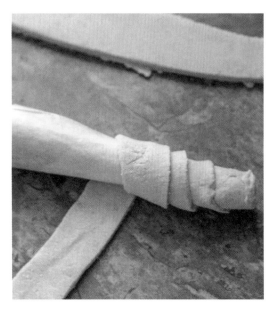

2. Wrap 3 strips around each cream horn mould, starting at the bottom.

3. Make sure each strip overlaps slightly so that the mould is completely covered.

4. The baked shell ready to fill.

Equipment

Baking paper
Rolling pin
6 cream horn moulds

For the filling

Heat a little oil in a pan and add the onion and sugar and fry until caramelised. Add the garlic and then the bacon and chicken and stir until cooked (see figure 5).

Push this to one side of the pan, add the butter to the other side and stir to melt. Add the cornflour and stir into the melted butter to make a roux (see figure 6).

Slowly pour in the milk, stirring so it doesn't get lumpy, and then slowly add the cream (see figure 3).

Add the mustard, cheddar cheese, spreadable cheese and pepper and stir until thoroughly mixed and the cheese has melted (see figure 4). Spoon the mixture evenly into the pastry cones to serve.

These pies are best eaten the same day, but you can store the cones unfilled in an airtight container for 3 days and the filling in the fridge in a covered bowl for 2–3 days if you wanted to make them up another day.

5. Fry the onion, sugar, garlic, bacon and chicken in a little oil until caramelised.

6. Melt the butter on one side of the pan and mix in the cornflour to make a roux.

7. Slowly pour in the milk, stirring to prevent lumps forming.

8. Stir in the mustard and cheeses until melted.

Little Cornish pasties

Makes 6   Difficulty rating

For the pastry
200 g (7 oz/1¹/₃ cups) plain
   (all-purpose) flour, plus a little
   extra for brushing
85 g (3 oz) butter, chilled, cut into
   small cubes
¹/₄ teaspoon salt
60 ml (2 fl oz/¹/₄ cup) cold water
60 ml (2 fl oz/¹/₄ cup) cold milk

For the filling
250 g (9 oz) minced
   (ground) beef
¹/₂ large onion, finely diced
125 g (4¹/₂ oz) swede, cubed
1 large baking potato, diced
1 egg, lightly beaten
Sea salt and freshly ground
   black pepper

Equipment
Food processor
12 cm (5 inch) round cutter
Pastry brush
Baking tray

Prep time: 10 minutes
Chilling time: 30 minutes
Baking time: 45–60 minutes

For the pastry
Put the flour and salt in a large bowl or food processor. Rub the butter into the flour with your hands or using the food processor, until it resembles course breadcrumbs. Add the water and milk and mix to form a firm dough. Roll the dough into a ball, cover with plastic wrap and refrigerate for 30 minutes.

Preheat the oven to 200°C/400°F.

For the filling
Put the meat and vegetables in a large bowl and toss through some seasoning.

Lightly dust a clean worktop with flour and roll out the pastry to around 5 mm (¹/₄ inch) thick. Cut out six 12 cm (5 inch) rounds. Arrange the filling evenly on one side of each round and brush a little of the beaten egg around the edge.

Lift the opposite edge of the pastry over the filling and press down to seal the pasty. Fold and pinch the dough around the edges to form a neat crimp.

Brush each pasty with egg to glaze and place on a baking tray. Bake for 45–60 minutes, or until golden and cooked through.

Cheddar beer pretzels

Makes 5 large pretzels   Difficulty rating

250 g (9 oz/1²/₃ cups) strong
    white flour
300 g (10¹/₂ oz/2 cups) plain
    (all-purpose) flour
1 teaspoon salt, plus extra
    for sprinkling
7 g (2 teaspoons) fast-action
    dried yeast
200 ml (7 fl oz) milk

100 ml (3¹/₂ fl oz) beer
40 g (1¹/₂ oz) butter, cubed
50 g (1³/₄ oz/¹/₂ cup) grated
    cheddar cheese
300 ml (10¹/₂ fl oz) water
1 tablespoon bicarbonate
    of soda (baking soda)

Equipment
Stand mixer
Baking tray
Baking paper
Pastry brush

Prep time: 30 minutes
Rising time: 1 hour
Baking time: 20–25 minutes

Put the flours, salt and yeast in the bowl of a stand mixer with a dough hook attached making sure the salt and yeast do not come into contact. Add the milk and beer and start kneading slowly. After about 2 minutes kneading, add the butter and cheese a little at a time and turn up the mixing speed. Continue kneading for 5 minutes.

Place the dough in a large oiled bowl, cover it with plastic wrap and leave to rise for 1 hour.

Once doubled in size, tip out onto a lightly floured surface and cut into 5 equal pieces. Roll the dough into long ropes and fold each one into a pretzel shape (see page 87). Place them on a lined baking tray. Preheat the oven to 200°C/400°F.

Bring the water to the boil in a saucepan and add the bicarbonate of soda. Brush some of this water onto each pretzel and then sprinkle on some salt.

Bake the pretzels for 20–25 minutes until golden brown. They are best eaten the same day, but will keep in an airtight container for 2 days.

SQUID INK BAGELS

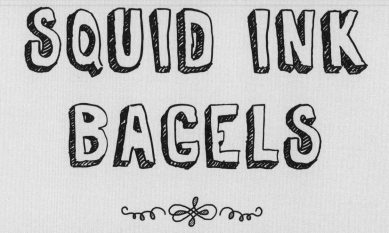

I know this sounds a little weird, but the squid ink adds
such a nice salty flavour to the bagels, and I promise they
don't taste fishy at all. Usually I would poach bagels
in a water bath for 30 seconds before baking them,
but this time I brushed on the water/baking soda mixture
and they turned out well. These inky black bagels are
perfect with salmon and cream cheese.

Squid ink bagels

Makes 10   Difficulty rating 🧤🧤

250 g (9 oz/1²/₃ cups) strong
    white flour
300 g (10¹/₂ oz/2 cups) plain
    (all-purpose) flour, plus
    extra for dusting
1 teaspoon salt, plus extra
    for sprinkling
7 g (2 teaspoons) fast-action
    dried yeast
200 ml (7 fl oz) milk
100 ml (3¹/₂ fl oz) warm water
4 x 5 ml sachets of squid ink
40 g (1¹/₂ oz) butter, chilled
    and cubed
300 ml (10¹/₂ fl oz) water
1 tablespoon bicarbonate
    of soda (baking soda)

Equipment
Stand mixer
Baking tray

Prep time: 30 minutes
Rising time: 1 hour 20 minutes
Baking time: 20–25 minutes

Put the flours, salt and yeast in the bowl of a stand mixer, making sure the salt and yeast do not come into contact. Add the milk, water and squid ink and start kneading slowly. After about 2 minutes kneading, add the butter a bit at a time and turn up the mixer. Continue kneading for 5 minutes.

Place the dough in a large oiled bowl, cover it with plastic wrap and leave to rise for 1 hour.

Once doubled in size, tip out onto a lightly floured surface and cut into 10 equal pieces. Flour your hands and roll each piece into a ball. Press your finger through the middle and spin the dough around to open the hole and make the bagel shape (see figures 1 to 3). Place them on a baking tray and leave for 20 minutes to prove.

Preheat the oven to 200°C/400°F.

Bring the water to the boil in a saucepan and add the baking soda. Brush some of this water onto each pretzel (see figure 4), then sprinkle on some salt. Bake the pretzels for 20–25 minutes or until when tapped on the base they sound hollow.

They are best eaten the same day, but can be stored in an airtight container for 2 days.

1. Press your finger through the middle of the dough ball.

2. Spin the dough around your finger to create the hole...

3. ... and create the bagel shape.

4. Brush each bagel with a little of the water and bicarbonate of soda mixture.

PEAR AND SALTED CARAMEL CHALLAH

I love making bread, especially challah. I was making
a pear challah and I was going to put honey in it,
then I changed my mind and used some salted caramel
sauce instead and it was lovely. If you don't have
any caramel sauce, try adding 150 ml /5 fl oz. of honey
and 180 ml/6 fl oz. water.

Pear and salted caramel challah

Makes 2   Difficulty rating 🧤🧤

450 g (1 lb/3 cups) strong
  white flour

3 eggs

1 teaspoon salt

60 g (2 oz/1/3 cup) soft light
  brown sugar

7 g (2 teaspoons) fast-action
  dried yeast

1 fresh rosemary sprig,
  finely chopped

4 tablespoons readymade
  salted-caramel sauce

80 g (2³/4 oz) butter

2 pears, finely chopped

50 g (1³/4 oz/1/4 cup)
  sliced almonds

1 egg, beaten

1 tablespoon milk

Pearl sugar and almonds;
  for dusting

Equipment

Food processor or stand mixer
Baking tray
Baking paper
Pastry brush

Prep time: 30 minutes
Rising time: 2 hours
Baking time: 35–45 minutes

Put the flour, eggs, salt, sugar, yeast, rosemary and salted caramel sauce in a bowl or a food processor, making sure to keep the salt and yeast separate. Mix for 2 minutes and then add the butter. Mix again for 1 minute and then add the pear and almonds. Mix for another 2 minutes.

Place the dough in a large oiled bowl, cover it with plastic wrap and leave to rise for 1 hour.

Once doubled in size, knock the air out of the dough and cut it into 3 pieces. Roll each piece out into ropes and then plait (see figures 1 to 4). Place the plaited loaf on a lined baking tray and leave to rise for another hour.

Mix the egg and milk together in a small bowl and brush onto the bread. Sprinkle on some pearl sugar and almonds.

Preheat the oven to 180°/350°F. Bake the challah for about 35–45 minutes or until golden and sounds hollow when tapped on the base. Leave to cool and then slice and enjoy. The challah is best eaten on the day but will keep for 3 days if covered.

1. Stick 3 ropes of dough together at the top.

2. Begin plaiting the 3 ropes, moving one rope over another to the middle, and then doing the same with the rope on the other side.

3. Keep plaiting the strands.

4. The finished plaited loaf.

FIG, HONEY, PISTACHIO AND GOAT'S CHEESE LOAF

❧❧❧❧❧❧

I love the flavours of this loaf – they all go together really well and the pistachios give it a great crunch. If you can't get any, then walnuts will work too.

Fig, honey, pistachio and goat's cheese loaf

Makes 1 loaf   Difficulty rating 🧤

Prep time: 40 minutes
Rising time: 1 hour 45 minutes
Baking time: 25 minutes

500 g (1 lb 2 oz/3⅓ cups)
  strong white flour
60 g (2 oz/⅓ cup) soft light
  brown sugar
2 teaspoons salt
7 g (2 teaspoons) fast-action
  dried yeast
100 ml (3½ fl oz) milk
1 egg, beaten
200 ml (7 fl oz) water
60 g (2 oz/¼ cup) butter
5 figs, sliced
125 g (4½ oz/⅓ cup)
  goat's cheese
3 tablespoons honey
20 pistachio nuts, chopped

Equipment
Stand mixer
Baking tray
Baking paper

Put the flour, sugar, salt and yeast in the bowl of a stand mixer with a dough hook attached (place the yeast on the opposite side of the bowl to the salt). Add the milk and beaten egg and start mixing. Slowly add the water and knead for 2 minutes. Add the butter and knead for a further 3–4 minutes. Place the dough in an oiled bowl, cover with plastic wrap and leave to rise for 1 hour.

Once the dough has doubled in size, knock the air out and roll into a large rectangle. Place the figs evenly over the dough and then crumble over the goat's cheese. Pour over some honey and scatter over the chopped pistachios (see figure 1).

Roll up the dough into a long log (see figure 2), then slice the dough down the centre making two long strands (see figure 3). Twist the two strands of dough together and shape into a circle (see figure 4).

Leave to prove on a lined baking tray for 45 minutes. Preheat the oven to 200°C/400°F. Bake for 25 minutes or until golden and sounds hollow when tapped on the base of the loaf.

1. Top the rolled out dough with figs, goat's cheese, honey and pistachios.

2. Start rolling from one long side to create a long log shape.

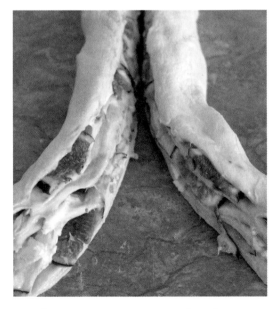

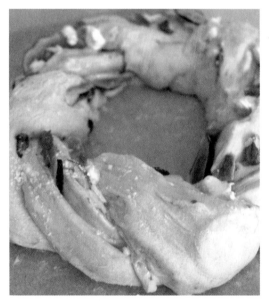

3. Slice down the centre of the long log to create two long strands of filled dough.

4. Weave the two strands of dough together and shape into a circle.

BEETROOT CHEDDAR FOUGASSE

A fougasse is a French version of the Italian focaccia.
I think it is a beautiful looking bread and is great served
with some oil for dipping. It's really easy to make,
although it's quite messy so it's best to knead
it in a stand mixer if you have one.

Beetroot cheddar fougasse

Makes 1 large loaf or 2 small loaves   Difficulty rating 🧤

250 g (9 oz/1²/₃ cups)
   strong white flour, plus
   extra for dusting
2 tablespoons beetroot powder
1 teaspoon salt
5 g (1 teaspoon) fast-action
   dried yeast
1 tablespoon olive oil, plus
   extra to finish
1 large cooked beetroot, puréed
150 ml (5 fl oz) cool water
50 g (1³/₄ oz/¹/₂ cup) grated
   cheddar cheese
Fine semolina, for dusting
   (optional)
Dried oregano, for sprinkling

Equipment
Stand mixer
Oiled bowl
Baking tray
Pizza cutter or sharp knife
Clean plastic bag

Prep time: 1 hour 20 minutes
Baking time: 15–20 minutes

Put the flour, beetroot powder, salt and yeast in the bowl of a stand mixer, making sure the salt and yeast do not come into contact. Add the oil, beetroot purée and three-quarters of the water and with the dough hook mix on a low to medium speed. Slowly add the rest of the water a bit at a time. Add the cheese and mix for a further 6–8 minutes, or until the dough becomes elastic and stretchy. Different brands of flour absorb water differently so you may need to add more or less water to get the right consistency. Tip the dough into an oiled bowl, cover it with plastic wrap and leave it to rise for 1 hour or until doubled in size.

Once the dough has risen, heavily flour the work surface and sprinkle over a layer of semolina, if using (it adds a nice crust to the bread). Gently tip the dough out – this dough does not require knocking back as you want to retain as much air as possible.

Gently shape the dough into a flat oval and place on a lined baking tray (see figure 1). Use a pizza cutter or sharp knife to cut lines in the dough to resemble a leaf (see figure 2). Gently stretch the dough to exaggerate the holes (see figures 3 and 4). Place the tray inside a clean plastic bag (making sure the bag is not touching the dough) and leave for 20 minutes while you preheat the oven to 220°C/425°F.

Spray the bread with olive oil, or drizzle it over the bread lightly, and sprinkle over the oregano. Bake for 15–20 minutes, or until the fougasse sounds hollow when tapped on the base. Leave to cool on a wire rack and eat within a few hours.

1. Shape the dough into a leaf shape on a baking tray.

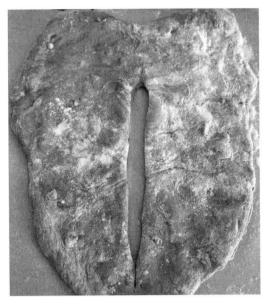

2. Use a pizza cutter or sharp knife to cut a slit down the centre of the dough.

3. Make other holes and use your fingers to stretch and exaggerate the dough to resemble a leaf pattern.

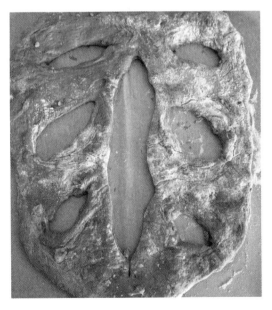

4. The finished fougasse shape before baking.

STENCILLED BUTTERMILK HONEY OAT LOAF

I wanted to do a flour stencil on bread, so I decided to try it on this buttermilk and honey loaf. I sprinkled oats around the edges of the loaf for decoration and added some into the loaf too.

Stencilled buttermilk honey oat loaf

Makes 1 loaf   Difficulty rating 🧤🧤

500 g (1 lb 2 oz/3¹/₃ cups)
   strong white flour, plus
   extra for dusting
7 g (2 teaspoons) fast-action
   dried yeast
1 tablespoon salt
2 ¹/₂ tablespoons honey
250 ml (9 fl oz/1 cup) buttermilk
125 ml (4 fl oz/¹/₂ cup) water
45 g (1¹/₂ oz) butter
30 g (1 oz) rolled oats,
   plus extra for sprinkling
Milk, for brushing

Equipment
Stand mixer
Oiled bowl
Plastic wrap
Stencil of choice

Prep time: 30 minutes
Rising time: 2 hours
Baking time: 35 minutes

Put the flour, yeast and salt in the bowl of a stand mixer fitted with the dough hook, making sure the salt and yeast do not come into contact. Add the honey, buttermilk and water and knead for 4 minutes. Add the butter and oats and continue kneading for a further 2–4 minutes. Alternatively, you can knead by hand if you don't have a stand mixer.

Put the dough in an oiled bowl, cover with plastic wrap and leave it to rise slowly overnight in the fridge – alternatively, you can let it rise at room temperature for at least an hour.

In the morning, leave the dough to sit at room temperature for 1 hour. Tip out onto a floured worktop and shape it as you wish – I decided to make a round loaf (see figure 1), but you can bake it in a tin if you prefer.

Brush the loaf with milk and place your chosen stencil on top. Sift over some flour (see figure 2). Remove the stencil and use a paintbrush to tidy up the pattern if needed (see figure 3). Sprinkle oats around the edge of the loaf. Place on a baking tray and set aside to prove for 30 minutes.

Preheat the oven to 180°C/350°F. Slash the dough with a blade around the edge (see figure 4) – this will stop the loaf from splitting on the top where you have the stencilled pattern. Bake for 35 minutes or until golden and sounds hollow when tapped on the base.

1. The proved dough shaped and ready for stencilling.

2. Place your chosen stencil on top of the dough and dust with flour.

3. Carefully remove the stencil to reveal the design.

4. Sprinkle oats around edge of loaf.

4. Little gifts

PARMESAN AND TOMATO BREADSTICK TWISTS

These breadsticks are full of flavour and a great addition to a buffet. They are based on Italian grissini but I divided the dough in half and added parmesan and herbs to one half and tomato purée and paprika to the other for an interesting flavour combination.

Parmesan and tomato breadstick twists

Makes 15 *Difficulty rating* 🧤

330 g (11³/₄ oz/2¹/₄ cups) plain
   flour, plus extra for dusting
7 g (2 teaspoons) fast-action
   dried yeast
200 ml (7 fl oz) milk
1 tablespoon salt
100 g (3¹/₂ oz) butter
3 tablespoons grated
   parmesan cheese
1 teaspoon dried oregano
¹/₄ teaspoon freshly ground
   black pepper
3 tablespoons tomato purée
1 teaspoon smoked paprika

Equipment
Food processor
Rolling pin
Baking tray

Prep time: 15–20 minutes
Baking time: 20 minutes

Put the flour, yeast, milk and salt in a food processor and mix then add the butter and mix until a ball of dough forms.

Cut the dough into 2 even balls. Put one back in the food processor and add the parmesan, oregano and black pepper and mix to combine. Remove the dough and place to one side while you flavour the next ball.

Put the other ball of dough in the food processor, add the tomato purée and paprika and mix to combine. Add 1 tablespoon flour if the purée makes the dough too moist.

Preheat the oven to 180°C/350°F.

Lightly dust a clean worktop with flour and shape both the doughs into equal rectangle shapes with your hands. Place one rectangle on top of the other and roll them out together (see figure 2) to make a layered larger rectangle about 40 x 30 cm (16 x 12 inches).

Slice the dough into 2 cm (1 inch) wide strips (see figure 3). Twist each one and place on a baking tray lined with baking paper (see figure 4).

Bake for 20 minutes until crisp. These breadsticks will keep in an airtight container for 2–3 days.

1. You will end up with two different coloured, even-sized balls of dough.

2. Layer the two doughs on top of each other and roll out.

3. Cut the dough into long thin strips.

4. Twist each strip before placing on the baking tray.

Homemade spelt flour spinach tortilla chips

Makes 8 tortillas and about 60 tortilla chips   *Difficulty rating* 🧤 🧤

For the tortillas
60 ml (2 fl oz/$^1/_4$ cup) water
3 packed cups of fresh spinach
3 tablespoons olive oil, plus
   more for spraying
$^1/_4$ teaspoon salt
250 g (9 oz/2 cups) spelt flour,
   plus extra for dusting
$^1/_4$ teaspoon baking powder

For the tortilla chips
$^1/_4$ teaspoon garlic herb
   seasoning (optional)
1 tablespoon sesame oil
   (or 2$^1/_2$ tablespoons olive
   oil if you prefer)

Equipment
Food processor
Baking tray
Frying pan
Oil spray bottle

Prep time: 15 minutes
Baking time: 20–25 minutes

For the tortillas
Put the spinach and water in a saucepan over a medium heat, put the lid on and cook for 7 minutes until the spinach has sweated down. Transfer the spinach to a food processor or blender with any water in the pan and purée.

Spoon the puréed spinach into a mixing bowl and add the oil, salt, three-quarters of the flour and the baking powder. Mix everything together, adding the rest of the flour slowly, until a soft ball of dough is formed.

Lightly dust a clean worktop with flour and divide the dough into 8 even balls. Roll each one out into tortilla shapes about 3 mm ($^1/_8$ inch) thick.

Dry-fry the tortillas in a hot frying pan for 35 seconds on each side. These tortillas can now be kept and used for sandwich wraps or to make chips continue with the next step of the recipe.

For the tortilla chips
Preheat the oven to 180°C/350°F.

Slice the tortillas into triangles and spread them out on a baking tray. Spray them all over with the oil and sprinkle over some garlic and herb seasoning and salt to flavour the chips. Bake for 6 minutes and then flip over and bake for a further 6 minutes. They will keep in an airtight container for 2–3 days.

Sweet potato cheddar crackers

Makes around 180 g/6 oz of crackers   *Difficulty rating* 🧤

110 g (3³/₄ oz/³/₄ cup) plain
  (all-purpose) flour, plus extra
  for dusting
¹/₂ teaspoon salt
1 teaspoon baking powder
¹/₄ teaspoon freshly ground
  black pepper
¹/₂ teaspoon smoked paprika
1 teaspoon chopped fresh chives
110 g (3³/₄ oz) grated
  cheddar cheese
1 tablespoon smoked
  spreadable cheddar cheese
  or soft cheese (optional)
125 g (4¹/₂ oz/¹/₂ cup) mashed
  sweet potato (approximately
  1 medium sweet potato)
30 ml (1 fl oz) milk

Equipment
Food processor
Baking paper
Rolling pin
Rotary pastry cutter
Baking tray

Prep time: 20 minutes
Resting time: 30 minutes
Baking time: 12–15 minutes

Put all the ingredients in a food processor and pulse until they come together into a ball.

Lightly dust a clean worktop with flour and tip the dough out. Knead together gently for 1 minute, wrap in plastic wrap and place in the fridge for 30 minutes.

Lay one big piece of baking paper on the worktop and dust with flour. Place the dough on top and then place a second piece of baking paper on top. Roll out with a rolling pin until 5 mm (¹/₄ inch) thick.

Use a rotary pastry cutter or pizza slice to cut out small rectangles and then use a fork to make holes in the dough. Place the crackers on a baking tray lined with baking paper and bake for 12–15 minutes until golden and puffed up. Eat straight away or store in an airtight container for 3–5 days.

Granola

Makes one 600 ml (21 fl oz) jar   Difficulty rating 🧤

185 g (6¹/2 oz) traditional
   rolled oats
75 g (2³/4 oz) unsweetened
   flaked coconut
120 g (4¹/2 oz/1 cup) coarsely
   chopped pecans or walnuts
60 g (2¹/4 oz/¹/4 cup)
   pumpkin seeds
65 g (2¹/2 oz/¹/4 cup)
   sunflower seeds
60 g (2¹/4 oz/¹/3 cup) soft light
   brown sugar
1 teaspoon ground cinnamon
¹/2 teaspoon freshly
   ground nutmeg
¹/4 teaspoon salt
80 ml (2¹/2 fl oz/¹/3 cup)
   maple syrup
45 g (1¹/2 oz) unsalted
   butter, melted
2 tablespoons melted
   coconut oil
2 teaspoons vanilla extract
3 tablespoons freeze-dried
   raspberries
35 g (1¹/4 oz/¹/4 cup) dried
   cranberries

Equipment
Baking tray
Baking paper
Storage jars

Prep time: 10 minutes
Baking time: 30 minutes

Preheat the oven to 160°C/325°F. Line a baking tray with baking paper and set aside.

Put the oats, coconut, pecans, seeds, brown sugar, cinnamon, nutmeg, and salt in a bowl and set aside.

Mix the maple syrup, melted butter, coconut oil and vanilla extract together in a small bowl.

Add the wet ingredients to the dry ingredients and mix together until all of the dry ingredients are moistened.

Spread the mixture out in an even layer over the prepared baking tray. Bake for 30 minutes, removing the pan from the oven every 10 minutes to stir and toss. The granola will be a deep golden brown when done. Remove from the oven and leave to cool completely, then mix in the dried fruit. It will keep in an airtight jar for 3 weeks.

 KNÄCKEBRÖD

These Swedish rye crispbreads are delicious
served with cream cheese. They are also perfect
to use with dips. They would make a great hostess
gift for a dinner party.

Knäckebröd

Makes 6   Difficulty rating 🧤

150 g (5¹/₂ oz/1¹/₄ cups) rye flour

150 g (5¹/₂ oz/1¹/₄ cups) spelt flour, plus extra for dusting

5 g (1 teaspoon) fast-action dried yeast

1 tablespoon cumin seeds

1 teaspoon sea salt

250 ml (9 fl oz/1 cup) warm water

Equipment
Food processor

Tea towel (dish towel)

Baking tray

Baking paper

Rolling pin

5 cm (2 inch) cookie cutter

Prep time: 10 minutes

Rising time: 30 minutes

Baking time: 1 hour

Mix both of the flours in a bowl and add the yeast, cumin seeds and salt. Slowly add the water a little at a time, mixing with your hands until you get a smooth dough. Alternatively, add the flour, yeast and salt to a food processor, mix together and then add the cumin seeds and water and mix until it comes together in a ball. Cover the bowl with a clean tea towel and leave to rise for 30 minutes.

Preheat the oven to 200°C/400°F and line a baking tray with baking paper.

Lightly dust a clean worktop with spelt flour and turn the dough out (see figure 1). Use your hands to roll the dough into a log shape. Cut the log into 6 equal pieces.

Take 2 of the dough pieces to start with and use a rolling pin to roll each one out to a roughly 15 cm (6 inch) diameter circle (see figure 2). Use a small 5 cm (2 inch) cookie cutter to cut a hole in the centre of each one (see figure 3). Use a fork to prick the remaining pastry with holes, before placing them on the baking tray (see figure 4).

Bake in the preheated oven for 15 minutes. Repeat with the other 4 dough pieces and then leave them all to cool on a wire rack. They will keep in an airtight container for 3–4 days.

1. Turn out the dough onto a floured worktop.

2. Roll out each dough ball to a 15 cm (6 inch) diameter circle.

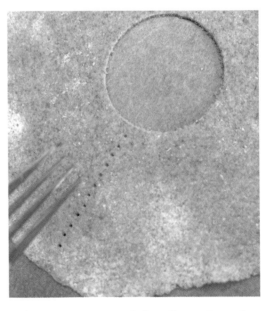

3. Cut a hole in the centre with a 5 cm (2 inch) cookie cutter.

4. Use a fork to prick holes all over the circle.

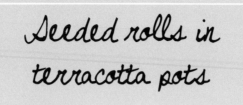

Seeded rolls in terracotta pots

Makes 5   Difficulty rating 🧤

100 g (3¹/₂ oz/²/₃ cup) strong
   white flour
200 g (7 oz/1¹/₃ cups) strong
   wholemeal flour
100 g (3¹/₂ oz/³/₄ cup) strong
   granary flour
2 tablespoons salt
7 g (2 teaspoons) fast-action
   dried yeast
30 g (1 oz) softened butter
250 ml (9 fl oz/1 cup) cold water
Olive oil, for kneading
2 teaspoons poppy seeds
2¹/₂ tablespoons pumpkin seeds,
   plus extra for sprinkling
2¹/₂ tablespoons sunflower seeds,
   plus extra for sprinkling
¹/₄ teaspoon chopped fresh
   rosemary, plus a few whole
   sprigs for topping the bread

Equipment
Oiled bowl
Plastic wrap
5 oiled plastic bags
5 clean terracotta pots
   (approx. 150 ml in volume)
Baking paper (optional)

Prep time: 10 minutes
Rising time: 1–2 hours and then 30 minutes
Baking time: 25–30 minutes

Put the flours in a large bowl and add the salt on one side of the bowl and the yeast on the other. Add the softened butter and three-quarters of the water. Mix together using your hands or in a stand mixer with a dough hook, then add the rest of the water. Mix until it comes together into a smooth dough.

Tip the dough out onto an oiled surface (use oil rather than flour to knead the dough with as kneading with flour can affect the recipe) or continue kneading with the stand mixer for about 5 minutes. Add the seeds and rosemary. Knead again until well combined. Continue to knead for 5 minutes until the dough becomes smooth. Place the dough in an oiled bowl, cover with plastic wrap and leave it to rise for 1–2 hours or until it has doubled in size.

Tip the dough out and knock out the air by folding it in on itself. Divide the dough into 5 equal pieces. Oil the terracotta pots or line them with baking paper. Put one ball of dough into each one, sprinkle some more seeds on top and add some rosemary sprigs. Loosely cover each with an oiled plastic bag and then set aside to rise again for 30 minutes.

Preheat the oven to 220°C/425°F. Place the pots on a baking tray and bake the risen dough for 25–30 minutes or until they turn a deep golden colour. These are best eaten on the day but can be kept in an airtight container for 1–2 days.

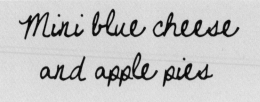

Mini blue cheese and apple pies

Makes 8   Difficulty rating 🧤

200 g (7 oz/1¹/₃ cups) plain (all-purpose) flour, plus extra for dusting
110 g (3³/₄ oz) unsalted butter, plus extra for brushing
1 egg yolk, plus another beaten egg for brushing
4–5 medium cooking apples
2¹/₂ tablespoons soft light brown sugar
20 g (³/₄ oz/1¹/₂ tablespoons) cornflour (cornstarch)
110 g (3³/₄ oz/½ cup) blue cheese
70 g (2¹/₂ oz/½ cup) walnuts

Equipment
Food processor
Rolling pin
Pastry brush

Prep time: 10 minutes
Resting time: 20 minutes
Baking time: 25 minutes

Put the flour and butter in a food processor and pulse to mix together. Add the egg yolk and continue to mix until a dough forms. Turn out of the mixer, cover with plastic wrap and transfer to the fridge for 20 minutes.

Preheat the oven to 180°C/350°F.

Peel and core the apples and chop into small pieces. Put the apple in a bowl and coat with the brown sugar and cornflour.

Crumble the blue cheese into the bowl and add the walnuts. Mix everything together so that it is all evenly distributed.

Lightly dust a clean worktop with flour and turn out the dough. Roll out the dough and cut into 16 circles. Brush the edges of half the circles with butter and then add the apple filling.

Top with another pastry circle, press the edges together, brush with a beaten egg and prick some holes in the top. Bake for 25 minutes until golden. These pies keep well in an airtight container for 3–4 days.

Baked camembert in filo pastry

Makes 1 / serves 4–5   Difficulty rating

60 g (2 oz/¼ cup) butter
5 sheets of filo pastry
1 camembert cheese
6 walnuts
2 tablespoons runny honey

Equipment
Baking tray
Baking paper
Tea towel

Prep time: 10 minutes
Baking time: 15–20 minutes

Preheat the oven to 180°C/350°F and line a baking tray with baking paper.

Melt the butter in a small saucepan. Cover the pastry sheets with a clean tea towel to stop them drying out.

Brush 1 sheet of filo pastry with butter and place it on the baking tray then repeat with another two sheets. Place the camembert on top, sprinkle on the nuts and drizzle over the honey. Bring the pastry sheets around and over the cheese.

Brush another two layers of pastry and place over the cheese then tuck the edges underneath so it looks neat.

Brush the top with more melted butter and bake for about 15–20 minutes or until golden.

MINI DARK CHOCOLATE AND ORANGE JELLY CAKES

These cakes are one of my favourite treats; they
are so moreish. They have a sponge base with a layer
of orange marmalade or jelly on top, and are
topped with chocolate.

1. Turn the sponge circles out onto a wire rack ready to top.

2. Spoon a little marmalade on top of each one.

3. Carefully dip each cake in melted chocolate.

4. Use a fork to make marks on the top of the chocolate to finish.

Mini dark chocolate and orange jelly cakes

Makes 12   Difficulty rating

For the sponge layer
60 g (2 oz/$1/4$ cup) butter
60 g (2 oz) caster
    (superfine) sugar
1 egg
60 g ($2^1/4$ oz) plain
    (all-purpose) flour
$1/2$ teaspoon baking powder
1 tablespoon milk

For the jelly layer
85 g (3 oz/$1/4$ cup) fine-cut
    marmalade

For the chocolate layer
125 g ($4^1/2$ oz) dark chocolate

Equipment
Silicone cupcake moulds
Cooling rack

Prep time: 10 minutes
Baking time: 10 minutes
Assembly time: 10 minutes

For the sponge layer
Preheat the oven to 180°C/350°F. Cream the butter and sugar together in a mixing bowl until pale. Add the egg and mix well. Sift the flour and baking powder into the bowl and fold in. Add the milk to loosen the batter a little and then spoon a tablespoon of batter into each hole of a cupcake mould and spread it out into a thin layer – it needs to be about 1 cm ($1/2$ inch) deep. Bake for about 10 minutes, remove from the moulds and leave to cool. If they rise a little in the oven, slice them into two to make them thinner.

To make the jelly layer
Put the marmalade in a small saucepan and heat up gently until it has melted. Spoon a little marmalade onto each sponge in a neat circle shape and then set aside to set.

Alternatively, spoon circles of marmalade onto a piece of baking paper and place it in the fridge to set. Use a palette knife to remove the jelly circles and slide them onto each sponge layer.

For the chocolate layer
Melt the chocolate in a glass bowl set over a pan of boiling water (making sure the water doesn't touch the base of the bowl).

Dip the top of each jelly-covered cake in the melted chocolate so that the surface is covered. Use a fork to make a pattern in the top of the chocolate, then set aside to harden. These cakes will keep in an airtight container for 3–5 days.

Pomegranate, pistachio and lemon biscotti

Makes 10   Difficulty rating 🧤

Prep time: 10 minutes
Baking time: 50 minutes

For the biscotti
85 g (3 oz) unsalted butter
125 g (4 1/2 oz) caster
    (superfine) sugar
2 eggs, beaten
Zest of 1 lemon and
    2 tablespoons juice
1 teaspoon vanilla extract
250 g (9 oz) plain
    (all-purpose) flour
3/4 teaspoon baking powder
Handful of chopped pistachios,
    plus a little extra for sprinkling
Handful of pomegranate seeds,
    plus a little extra for sprinkling

For the icing
2 teaspoons lemon juice
75 g (2 3/4 oz) icing
    (confectioners') sugar

Equipment
Baking tray
Baking paper

For the biscotti
Preheat the oven to 180°C/350°F and line a baking tray with baking paper.

Cream the butter and sugar together until pale and creamy. Add the eggs, making sure you scrape down the sides of the bowl as you go. Add the lemon juice and zest and vanilla extract and then sift in the flour and baking powder. Fold in the chopped pistachios and pomegranate seeds.

Use floured hands to shape the mixture into a log shape and place on the lined baking tray. Flatten the log a bit and sprinkle on some more chopped pistachios and pomegranate seeds.

Bake for 35 minutes. Remove from the oven and leave to cool for 5 minutes until it is cool enough to handle. Turn the oven down to 170°C/325°F.

Slice the biscotti into thin diagonal pieces and place them cut side up on the baking tray. Bake for a further 15 minutes until lightly golden and crisp. Leave to cool on a wire rack while you make the icing.

For the icing
Mix the lemon juice with the icing sugar and drizzle a little over each biscotti. These biscotti will keep for 1 week in an airtight container.

WALNUT BAKLAVA

Baklava is delicious — my mum introduced me to it, having discovered her own love for it when she lived in Greece for a little while in her early twenties after completing her nurse training. I love to bake it for her as it's her favourite treat.

Walnut baklava

Makes about 30 pieces   Difficulty rating

Prep time: 20 minutes
Baking time: 25 minutes
Cooking time: 10 minutes

For the baklava
250 g (9 oz/1½ cups) walnuts
110 g (3¾ oz) butter
1 x 220 g pack of filo pastry

For the syrup
60 g (2 oz) caster
   (superfine) sugar
1 tablespoon rose water
1 tablespoon orange-
   blossom water
⅛ teaspoon ground cinnamon
60 ml (2 fl oz/¼ cup) water

For the decoration
Candied and fresh unsprayed/
   organic rose petals to
   decorate if desired

Equipment
Food processor
Tea towel
Baking tin
Baking paper
Pastry brush

For the baklava
Preheat the oven to 180°C/350°F and line a rectangular baking tin with baking paper (see figure 1). Put the nuts in a food processor and pulse a few times to chop. Do not over process them, as you want them to remain in small chunks.

Melt the butter in a small pan over a gentle heat. Cover the pastry with a tea towel to stop it drying out. Take a sheet of pastry and brush it with the melted butter (see figure 2). Fold the pastry to fit into the tin. Brush three more layers of pastry with butter and place into the tin, then spread over half the nuts (see figure 3). Continue adding another three layers of pastry and then add the remaining nuts, reserving a small amount to sprinkle on top.

Finally, add three more layers, ensuring that each one is brushed with butter. Brush the top layer with more butter and then use a sharp knife to slice into squares, right the way through to the bottom of the pastry. Sprinkle with some more nuts (see figure 4), then bake for 25 minutes until golden and crisp.

For the syrup
Put all the syrup ingredients in a pan over a gentle heat and stir until the sugar has dissolved. Let it to continue to cook and reduce for 5 minutes. Brush some water around the sides of the pan to stop the syrup from burning.

Once the baklava has cooled down, pour the syrup over it – do not do this while it is still warm or you will make the baklava soggy. It will keep for 1 week in an airtight container.

1. Line a baking tray with baking paper and get your ingredients ready.

2. Lay a sheet of pastry in the base of the baking tray and brush with melted butter.

3. Spread over half the chopped nuts to cover the pastry in an even layer.

4. Use a sharp knife to slice the pastry into squares and top each with a sprinkle of chopped nuts.

Maple-roasted and cinnamon sugar pecans

Makes 300 g (10 oz) jar   Difficulty rating 🧤

Prep time: 5 minutes
Baking time: 25 minutes (maple pecans) and
  1 hour (cinnamon pecans)

For the maple-roasted pecans
45 g (1¹/₂ oz) butter
4 tablespoons soft light
  brown sugar
4 tablespoons maple syrup
300 g (10¹/₂ oz/3 cups)
  pecan halves

For the cinnamon sugar pecans
1 egg white (you will only
  need half)
1 tablespoon water
¹/₂ teaspoon vanilla extract
110 g (4 oz/¹/₂ cup)
  granulated sugar
1 teaspoon ground cinnamon
Pinch of salt
220 g (8 oz/2¹/₄ cups)
  pecan halves

Equipment
Baking tin
Baking paper
Wire rack

For the maple-roasted pecans
Preheat the oven to 180°C/350°F and line a baking tray with baking paper.

Melt the butter in a saucepan over a gentle heat. Add the sugar and maple syrup. Stir in the nuts to coat them, then spread them out onto a lined baking tray (discarding any leftover maple and butter mixture).

Bake for 15 minutes, then remove the tray from the oven, mix the nuts and stir them around. Turn the oven down to 150°C/300°F and bake for a further 10 minutes. Remove the nuts from the tray and place onto a wire rack to cool and dry. They will keep in an airtight container for about 2 weeks.

For the cinnamon sugar pecans
Preheat the oven to 130°C/250°F. In a large mixing bowl, whisk together half an egg white with the water and vanilla until frothy.

In a separate small mixing bowl, mix together the sugar, cinnamon and salt. Add the pecans to the egg white mixture and toss until evenly coated. Pour half the sugar mixture over the pecans and toss several times. Add the remaining sugar mixture and toss until evenly coated.

Pour the coated pecans over a lined baking sheet and spread into an even layer. Bake in the preheated oven for 1 hour, stirring every 15 minutes. Allow to cool, then store in an airtight container for up to 2 weeks.

ACKNOWLEDGEMENTS

I would like to dedicate this book to my mum who inspired me to start baking and has always been so encouraging. I would also like to thank my partner Howard, who was such a great help to me whilst I was writing this book, as well as Jan from Maddocks Farm Organics.

For more recipes and inspiration, please visit my blog at twiggstudios.com

INDEX

Published in 2016 by Murdoch Books, an imprint of Allen & Unwin

Copyright © Elwin Street Productions 2016
Conceived and produced by
Elwin Street Productions
3 Percy Street
London W1T 1DE
elwinstreet.com

Murdoch Books Australia
83 Alexander Street
Crows Nest NSW 2065
Phone: +61 (0) 2 8425 0100
Fax: +61 (0) 2 9906 2218
murdochbooks.com.au
info@murdochbooks.com.au

Murdoch Books UK
Erico House, 6th Floor
93–99 Upper Richmond Road
Putney, London SW15 2TG
Phone: +44 (0) 20 8785 5995
murdochbooks.co.uk
info@murdochbooks.co.uk

For Corporate Orders & Custom Publishing contact
Noel Hammond, National Business Development Manager, Murdoch Books Australia

Photographer: Aimee Twigger

A cataloguing-in-publication entry is available from the catalogue of
the National Library of Australia at nla.gov.au.

ISBN 978 1 74336 625 7 Australia
ISBN 978 1 74336 742 1 UK

A catalogue record for this book is available from the British Library.

IMPORTANT: Those who might be at risk from the effects of salmonella poisoning (the elderly,
pregnant women, young children and those suffering from immune deficiency diseases) should consult their doctor
with any concerns about eating raw eggs.

DISCLAIMER: Individuals using or consuming the flowers and plants listed in this book do so entirely at their own
risk. Always check a reputable source to ensure that the plants you are using are non-toxic, organic, unsprayed and
safe to be consumed. The publisher cannot be held responsible for any adverse reactions.

OVEN GUIDE: You may find cooking times vary depending on the oven you are using. For fan-forced ovens, as a
general rule, set the oven temperature to 20°C (35°F) lower than indicated in the recipe.